GAMES FOR ENGLISH LITERATURE

GAMES FOR ENGLISH LITERATURE

Izabela
Hopkins

and

David
Roberts

First published in 2016 by Libri Publishing

Copyright © Libri Publishing

Authors retain copyright of individual chapters.

The right of Izabela Hopkins and David Roberts to be identified as the authors of this work has been asserted in accordance with the Copyright, Designs and Patents Act, 1988.

ISBN 978-1-909818-89-7

A CIP catalogue record for this book is available from The British Library

Design and cover by Carnegie Book Production

Printed in the UK by Short Run Press

Libri Publishing
Brunel House
Volunteer Way
Faringdon
Oxfordshire
SN7 7YR

Tel: +44 (0)845 873 3837

www.libripublishing.co.uk

Contents

Author Biographies

Izabela Hopkins obtained her PhD from Birmingham City University on the subject of whiteness in American fiction. Her teaching and research interests include literary theory and the intersections between literature, identity and place. She is a Visiting Lecturer in the School of English at Birmingham City University and in the Institute of Humanities and Creative Arts at University of Worcester.

David Roberts is Professor of English and Dean of the Arts, Design and Media at Birmingham City University. A widely published theatre historian and literary critic, his recent books include *Restoration Plays and Players* and *Thomas Betterton,* both for Cambridge University Press. He also writes programme essays for the Royal Opera House and in 2013 was awarded a National Teaching Fellowship by the UK Higher Education Academy.

Acknowledgements

We would like to thank the students of Birmingham City University who have played some of our games. Gareth Courage has worked with us on materials for a high-concept board game called *Monstrosity* which we hope will see the light of day soon. David Roberts's award of a National Teaching Fellowship and Innovative Pedagogies Funding from the UK Higher Education Academy made it possible to undertake the research for this book. Special thanks go to Fiona Shaw Roberts and Dee Gough.

Learning Combined with Diversion

Theory

> Learning combined with diversion has a very different effect
> from instruction. Faced with a range of games, the student
> becomes more ready to engage, to derive amusement from the
> very process of learning. In a state that could be described as
> good humour, the student begins to learn without any obstacles
> of duress or reluctance.

You might imagine those are the words of a contemporary learning
and teaching guru celebrating the role of e-games in the curriculum:
a vividly post-chalk-and-talk call to pedagogic arms. In fact, they are
a translation of ideas set to paper in 1777 by a Polish writer called
Michał Dymitr Tadeusz Krajewski. In his compendiously entitled book,
*Educational games for children serving to facilitate their education,
through which they can easily learn letters, spelling, reading in Polish
and French, writing, history, geography and rudimentary arithmetic, and
have their character formed*, Krajewski set out to show that games, far
from being a frivolous distraction – the thing that starts in the breaks
when learning stops – are a teacher's greatest asset.

So, the idea that games promote learning is a longstanding one.
Engaging, competitive and goal-oriented, they provide students
with the chance to learn through doing, and teachers with a

heaven-sent opportunity to set tasks that are fun to complete on their own terms. Enjoyment of play is part of being human, a diversion that enhances the cognitive potential of the player, promoting an active approach to learning whereby students learn by doing. Games, Krajewski argued, could be adapted to suit the age of the learner, and the scholar-friendly atmosphere created by an environment of play serves to counteract the relative tedium of more established methods.

Since Krajewski, of course, the technology of games has moved on. Now, many academics who write about games pedagogy are concerned with multiplying literacies. In a world where the printed book is challenged by hand-held devices, X-Boxes and PlayStations, how are we to balance the competing demands and attractions of such different platforms? What counts as literacy now? And how can the use of games – so often the product of new technologies – help us to improve teaching when the world is awash with them? It's a question largely avoided by most teachers of English Literature, who have resisted using games partly because there is a natural playfulness in the acts of reading and interpretation, and partly because there is an abundance of published material on how to use creative activities in the English classroom. But creative activities do not have the same elements of fun and competition that have made games so attractive to educators since Tadeusz Krajewski. There is no reason why games cannot be used to stimulate an interest in the core concerns of English Literature.

To some, the effort would be pointless. Some writers go as far as to argue that we should abandon the traditional English curriculum of more or less canonical texts and focus instead on the language interactions stimulated by *Grand Theft Auto* or *World of Warcraft*. Others focus on the way digital animation and other graphic narratives offer space to critique the strategies people use to make sense of *Treasure Island* or *Noughts and Crosses*. There is a prevailing tendency among people who write about games to view them under the sign of what is now called 'literacy studies'.[1]

That field is a stroke of the pen away from the focus of this book, which you might say is radically traditional in two ways. Our interest is in *literary* studies: in the understanding, that is, of how (mostly) printed narratives, poems and plays are formed, structured, contextualized and interpreted. As far as games are concerned, we're not particularly interested in hi-tech immersive software, which is expensive to design and relatively short in lifespan. Instead, we give prominence to games that can be played with relatively simple materials: sets of cards, dice, boards, and so on.

But none of our games is an end in itself. Their purpose is not to reveal some pre-existing set of data or answers. Like the study of literature, they are designed as provocations to discovery, to independent and collective thought, to a more sophisticated grasp and use of language. In his great book of 1938, *Homo Ludens,* the social historian Johan Huizinga concluded that the evolution of the game was crucially linked to the development of civic institutions. In the rhetorical curriculum of Renaissance grammar schools sat the principle that games were an expression of verbal mastery, enjoyable but completely non-trivial, and anything but pre-determined in their outcome. For more detail on the philosophical justification for our approach here, we refer you to an article we've published in the 2015 volume of the journal *Changing English*.[2]

The games in this book are designed to be adaptable to different levels of study. Some are more likely to appeal more to 'A' level students than to undergraduates, and vice versa. They draw on a common stock of materials that can be bought and adapted at little cost, and in some cases they map directly onto the kind of questions

---

1   See, for example, Peter Bennett, Alex Kendall and Julian McDougall, *After the Media. Culture and Identity in the 21st Century* (London: Routledge, 2011); Andrew Burn, 'Potter-Literacy – from book to game and back again; literature, film, game and cross-media literacy', in *Papers: Explorations into Children's Literature*. Vol 14, No 2 (2004), pp 5-17, and the same author's 'Multi-text Magic: Harry Potter in book, film and videogame', in Collins, F. and Ridgman, J., eds., *Turning the Page: Children's Literature in Performance and the Media* (Bern: Peter Lang, 2006).

2   Hopkins and Roberts, 'Chocolate-covered Broccoli? Games and the teaching of literature', *Changing English*, vol.22 no.2 (2015), pp.222-36.

that typically get asked when students face assessment. Many of the games can be played without a teacher being present, although many also assume that someone will be there to draw together threads of discussion. If nothing else, experience tells us that these games are a great way of overcoming that horrible problem, the wall of silence, that confronts every teacher of literature at some stage in his or her career. We hope that you and your students find these games a great stimulus to engagement, argument and understanding.

Our games are divided into different categories, reflecting the way literature students have to move between detailed analysis and general evaluation. We start small, with games about words and images, and build towards the more challenging theoretical topics students might encounter in the study of literary theory. There is a fair but not equal representation of games in each category, and of course some games could be assigned to more than one. The final chapter considers the trans-disciplinary matter of designing games to promote argument. It is our hope that this section will encourage teachers in other disciplines to think about how they teach extended texts of whatever type. Overall, this book is conceived as a provocation, not an encyclopaedia. If the result is that readers go away and dream up more and better games to play with students of literature, history, sociology, law, or any other discipline involving the close study and theorization of texts, it will have served its purpose.

Each game is presented in a common format: purpose, accessories, process, outcomes/reflections, and variations. In some cases there are extended reflections on the methodological or philosophical issues raised. Readers will undoubtedly want to practise first before trying out the games on a class. In the early phases of each category, examples are given of the kind of cards or material that might be used, as a prompt. Once you get the hang of it, you can make your own choices depending on what you think are the priorities or themes you wish to pursue.

Practicalities

It's tempting to think that a game must be glossily designed to be appealing. Not necessarily. A little DIY can go a long way towards introducing variety into your classroom. A lot depends on motivating students to work in teams and adopt a 'pub quiz' approach, awarding points and prizes as you go but balancing the simplicity of that approach with manifest complexity of ideas and engagement. Some of the best games we've tried can be prepared using nothing more than a pair of scissors and a photocopier. One of the great advantages of using games to teach literature is the process of 'defamiliarizing' the text: inviting students to look at it from different perspectives or, more simply, just cutting it up into fragments. You could try this with, for example, a Shakespeare sonnet.

Make some photocopies of the poem (try no.29 – 'When in disgrace' – for starters), cut them into fourteen pieces (one per line), jumble up the pieces, put the students in groups and ask them to put the pieces back together in the right order, either against the clock or with points for the winning group. Then discuss the decisions they made along the way and explore the cohesive patterns of the poem. How much is repetition, and how much moves the argument forward? Do the gear changes happen where you would expect (at the end of a quatrain, etc)? What key words or images leap out? This approach forces students to attend to detail in ways they had not envisaged before and encourages them to view the text as a made, crafted entity that can be disassembled. For a variant on the game, slice the sonnet into three quatrains and the concluding couplet but give them only the couplet to start with. Ask them to figure out what train of thinking led up to it. Then feed them the quatrains randomly and see if they can put them in the right order, reflecting on how their assumptions about the argument matched what Shakespeare wrote. The groups then agree on who got closest to Shakespeare and award points accordingly.

For creative variants, try withholding the couplet and run a competition to see which group can write the best conclusion to the three quatrains. Then share the real version and assess how far it explores territory the students didn't imagine. Alternatively, withhold individual lines or words and run a similar competition. Shakespeare sonnets have been chosen as an example here but of course you can play similar games for any short poem, however clearly or mysteriously structured.

Designing

All the games contained in this guidebook use simple ludic ingredients in various combinations: counters, dice, cards and boards. Designing a new set of accessories for every game would be both time consuming and cost ineffective. Simplicity of design and, whenever feasible, recyclability of accessories are key to avoiding escalating cost and effort. With every change of rules, the game changes: reason enough not to underestimate the potential of ludic recycling or piggybacking.

Not all accessories will lend themselves easily to recycling. While a generic board may be adapted to different game scenarios, the same cannot be said of cards, which tend to be more game specific. The first step, of course, is to design a versatile board: we suggest basing it on a simple *Ludo* or *Monopoly*-type board, with a track round the outside, places for cards, converging tracks as necessary. With all these games, we're aiming for a correspondence between its layout, content and the projected cognitive outcomes. It may take several attempts to get this right, so try not to get discouraged. Regardless of how much time and effort it may take you to design a generic board, you will come out victorious with a ready tool to be used and reused at will; the reward is worth the initial outlay.

Once you have overcome all the conceptual hurdles and hold a prototype of a working board, it's time to dust off your artistic skills and put theory into practice. The simplest and cheapest way to produce your own board is to draw it yourself. All it takes are a ruler, coloured markers and, ideally, a colour photocopier on which it can be reproduced on A3 paper. These resources are readily available at most institutions. Even if you have to purchase stationery, with prices starting from about £5 for a pack of four markers and £5.99 for a pack of twelve sheets of A3 card, the financial outlay will be modest (the spontaneity of the design will add to the informal character of the game and may even act as an icebreaker). If, however, you're reluctant to expose your drawing skills to public scrutiny, you do not require an expensive graphic design software to achieve your goal.

Excelling

You will find the basic tools for drawing in Microsoft Excel, which comes with the standard MS Office package. Begin by opening a new spreadsheet and right clicking on a selected number of cells depending on the desired size of squares. Highlight the selection, right click on it and then select 'Format Cells' from the drop down menu. This will allow you to put a border around the cells, turning them into a neat square. Repeat the process until you have reached the required number of squares. Alternatively, you may access the border menu by clicking on the 'Border' icon on your toolbar. If you wish to insert text into the bordered area, highlight it as before and right click on it. Select again 'Format Cells' and then from the tabs at the top, click on 'Alignment'. Once there, select 'Merge cells', which will remove the grid lines from the square, adding a touch of aesthetic neatness. In order to type text within the already marked space, simply double click on the square. The text within the square may be manipulated by right-clicking on the square, selecting 'Alignment' and then choosing the options that best suit your purpose. To enhance the aesthetic quality of the board further, you may wish to insert pictures and shapes, all of which may be quickly accomplished by clicking on the 'Insert' tab and then the 'Picture' or 'Shapes' icon. Once you click on the desired object, it'll be automatically inserted in the spreadsheet, leaving you to drag it and secure its position within the confines of the square. You can adjust the size of the inserted object (and the square as well) by simply clicking on it, placing the cursor over one of the small square or circular icons that you will see on its outline and then dragging to expand or contract the image. Instead of right clicking on the cell selection, you may also access the alignment option by accessing

'Merge and Centre' tab in the Menu section at the top of the spreadsheet. To inject a little colour into your board, just highlight the required cells and click on the 'Fill' icon in the 'Font' section of the toolbar, where you will be able to choose from a variety of fixed colours or create a new one.

Excel does not stop there. You don't even need to limit yourself to rectangular or square boards. A circular board may be designed very quickly by following these simple steps.

- Open an Excel spreadsheet and click on 'Insert' in the Menu bar.
- Select 'SmartArt', which will open a list of graphics available.
- Choose 'Cycle' from the list.
- A cycle in a frame will automatically be inserted in your spreadsheet.
- Hover the cursor over a corner of the frame until an arrow appears, then click on it and stretch. Repeat the procedure for each corner.
- Select any circle in the diagram by clicking on it and then click on 'Add Shape' in the top left corner of the screen.
- Continue until the desired number of circles has been added.
- To add text to circles, simply click on each circle and type in the message.
- To change the colour of a circle, right click on it and select 'Format Shape' which is the last option on the list.

Right clicking on each circle will also enable you to change shapes and fonts, cut and paste, as well as expand your diagram by adding additional circles.

It may seem like hard work, but having a ready-made template has the additional advantage of allowing you to make changes to the board quickly and at minimal effort. It will also mean having a convenient tool in your arsenal which is available at the click of a button. To make the board more durable than the standard 80 or 90gsm copier paper affords, you could opt for printing on card. The cost of 12 sheets of A3 white card is around £5.99 – a small price to pay to ensure reusability.

Since the emphasis is on reusability and thus versatility, it may be worth investing in having your board printed professionally and laminated to eliminate wear and tear. Your institution's printing department should be your first port of call; alternatively, a local printer should be able to help. Depending on the printing process, prices range from £2 to £6 for an A3 size poster. Laminating is more expensive with prices around £10 per A3 one-sided sheet. Although outsourcing is a relatively expensive option, many places offer discounts on multiple copies and the end product is likely to justify the means. This may have the familiar ring of the well-worn quality vs. quantity argument but with an important caveat added: playability over quality. As long as the board is clear and consonant with the game instructions, your game will be playable regardless of the quality of the paper that went into its printing.

Unlike the boards, cards are easier to design but their reusability will be dictated by changes to the curriculum. There is always a handful of texts and themes that persistently return every year and these are the obvious target when it comes to reusability. With others, it is literally back to the drawing board. Depending on the mechanics and the outcome of the game, you may wish to implement different card categories designated, for example, by discrete colours. Looking at a deck of playing cards will give you an idea of the size your cards should be. This is the size we opted for in the design of our games and found it both sufficient to contain the requisite information and small enough to be placed in the centre of the board whenever rules demanded it. Handwriting is always an option, but in this case we would not recommend it for fear it may compromise legibility, not to mention make the enterprise more time consuming and the result less effective. By far the quickest and simplest option would be to design your cards using Microsoft Office Publisher.

Publishing

Begin by opening a new document in MS Office Publisher. At first glance, it may seem quite formidable, but first impressions are often wrong. Opening a new document will also open a 'Format

Publication' window which will be visible on the left-hand side of your screen. From there, proceed to click on 'Change Paper Size' button. This will take you to the next screen from which you will be able to select or customise an existing template. By clicking on the selection name (we usually opt for 'Business Cards'), you will narrow your search considerably. This will bring up a list of options to choose from. All templates contain sizes, thus further simplifying the process. Regardless of which option you select, you will be able to adjust the measurements of the card by following the instructions which will appear in the window in the top right corner of your screen. Once you have selected a template, its enlarged version will appear on the screen and you may begin typing immediately. When finished, save the card and then click on the 'Add to Content Library' icon located between the 'Paste' and 'Format Painter' icons. Once the card has been added to the library, the 'Library Content' window will appear on the left hand side of the screen. The process needs to be repeated only once for each category, regardless of the number of cards contained therein. To select a card for printing, simply click on it in the 'Library Content' window. The MS Office Publisher will populate the card on a sheet of standard paper, unless otherwise stipulated, as many times as its size allows. The yield is likely to be between 6 and 8 cards per sheet of A4 paper. And you are not limited to text only but may add text boxes, objects or pictures. Simply click on the 'Insert' tab and explore your options. Right clicking on each card held in the 'Library Content' will allow you to edit it at any time in the future – rather handy should revisions be required. All that remains to be done is arm yourself with coloured paper which, at £5.49 per 100 sheets of one colour, is likely to keep you well stocked for a considerable time. The same goes for the purchase of counters and dice which, currently priced at £ 5.57 for an assorted pack of 40 and £0.95 for a pack of 10 respectively, may be found on Amazon.

So, a little creative ingenuity and willingness to experiment are all it takes to break out of the confines of routine and inject a little variety into your classroom. All that remains is to be said is 'Let the games begin'.

1

Games about Words and Images

i. 'What's the connection?'

Purpose and Aims

To promote close engagement with literary texts through emphasis on word choices. This activity invites the students to examine the interrelationship between words and meaning and the ways in which both may be manipulated to influence interpretation.

Accessories

Excerpts, paper, marker pens.

Process

The students are divided into groups and each group is presented with a passage from a given text relating to, for example, a different character (you'll need to write the name of the character at the top of the passage). First, students identify the key words or phrases they deem crucial to the construction of this character. Then, they have to re-construct the character by rewriting and/or editing the fragment, without using the key words. Each group presents the reconstructed characters to the other groups, without revealing their names. The group or groups who guess the identity of the character are awarded a point each. After each presentation, the group has to explain what prompted their selection of particular words: was it prior knowledge of the story, or a reflection of contemporary standards, or something else? The game helps demonstrate how readers' perceptions of characters may be altered or manipulated through language.

Outcomes and Reflections

Note the instances of repetition of lexical choices in the presentations and initiate a discussion of what may have prompted them. Such reflection combined with a close analysis of text will further illustrate the link between lexis and social and cultural assumptions that permeate literary texts

Variations

Although this is a more prescriptive version, it still leaves the students enough room to be creative and meets the objectives of the game. In this scenario, the students substitute the identified words and phrases with their polar opposites, effectively turning heroes into villains and vice versa. The remainder of the activity proceeds as above.

To make the game more complex, try branching out to analyse language in relation to place or setting. The students work in groups and each group is given a passage as well as a set of characters from a given text. First, they are to identify the words crucial to the construction of the setting and substitute words of their choice for them. Next, looking at the list of characters, they must decide who would be at home and who out of place in this setting. They present their findings to the rest of the class. The word choices of the group will determine which characters will be at home and which out of place, leading to a discussion of theoretical concepts of marginality and centrality, for example.

ii. Word associations

Purpose and Aims

To foster inter-textual and inter-contextual associations. The game helps the students to consolidate information and solidify their existing knowledge.

Accessories

Thematic cards, a timer, blank sheets of paper, markers.

Process

This game requires a minimum of two players/teams, an adjudicator, and a stack of cards featuring prompts to suit the theme you wish to explore. For the adjudicator, choose one of the more able students in the class. So, if the set text is Jane Austen's *Pride and Prejudice* the cards might offer relatively obvious character or setting-based prompts such as 'Uncle Gardiner', 'Derbyshire', or 'London', or ones relating to narrative format such as 'letters' or 'third person', or more conceptual and argumentative ones: 'money', 'didactic', 'pastoral', 'post-revolutionary', or 'conservative', for example. You could even use pictures. Try to include some really far-fetched (but not impossible) prompts to stretch students' ingenuity. You could even duplicate some cards to see what different responses they provoke.

The first player/team picks up a card from a deck and places it face up to one side. The next player/team picks up a card and decides whether it matches the card already on the table. Set the timer for the decision, depending on how intense you want the game to be or how complex the prompts. The adjudicator decides whether the 'match' is valid; the emphasis is on the players or teams to come up with a convincing explanation. If there is no match, the player/team has to keep the card. Since the criteria for matches may potentially change with every move as new information is added, the game remains dynamic throughout. The player/team left with fewest cards at the end of the round wins.

Outcomes and Reflections

Afterwards, you could try this. Each pair or group takes stock of the left over cards and prepares a presentation explaining why these cards have not been utilised. Since the unused cards will largely differ from group to group, the presentations not only provide feedback but also enhance the students' existing knowledge. And, in reversing the procedure, the students continue to build their confidence in building arguments and critical thinking.

iii. Semi-automatic writing

Purpose and Aims

To aid creative thinking and stimulate reflection on the process of composition. The activity allows the students to engage with the two aspects of literary production: creative output and criticism.

Accessories

Cards with words and/or pictures, timer.

Process

Cut up a short poem (something like Philip Larkin's 'Days', or you could just take a verse from a longer poem) into single words, like fridge vocabulary. Challenge the students to put them in the right order. Use a timer; first group to give the correct answer wins. Then discuss what the clues were. Show them the correct version and discuss how some of the wrong choices were creative in their own way. Then (really interesting part), ask them to produce a new poem using the same words, or with up to six that are different, substituted one for one. As an extra, supply a picture prompt to get them thinking about a particular theme.

Outcomes and Reflections

The students read out their poems to the rest of the class and explain what purpose the recycled words serve. They may turn to the original poem to furnish parallels or contrasts in structure, tone, and so on.

Variations

Students analyse a re-assembled version of the poem before they are presented with the correct version and then compare the two. This could lead to a discussion of patterns of meaning and creative process. For the second part of the exercise, ask them to jumble the words up and put them in an envelope. The students then take turns in pulling out the words and placing them next to one another. This part of the exercise becomes a foray into automatic writing and an exploration of a creative technique. To add extra variety, have the students use different picture prompts but the same poem.

iv. A sort of puzzle

Purpose and Aims

To work closely with a text. This game follows the logic of a puzzle and, beginning at the level of a word and moving to composition, it helps the students to develop lexical alertness while consolidating knowledge of a given text.

Accessories

Word cards, cards with sentences, timer, excerpts from a text.

Process

Students are divided into groups and given a number of cards containing a single word each. The words come from a single text and deal, for example, with the description of a particular character. The students examine the cards and decide to which character they may apply. Next, they are given a number of cards containing sentences. Again, they decide to which character they may refer. This should stimulate them to seek correspondences or discordances between the single word descriptions and the longer ones. Once they've settled on a name, they are given a passage from this particular text minus the words and sentences which they've already received on cards. Their task is to decide where these words and phrases fit in the passage. Time the exercise and award points for the group that gets there first.

Outcomes and Reflections

To initiate a general debate, the groups draw lots and only one group presents the 'finished' passage to the rest of the class. They explain how they chose the character and the rationale behind completing the passage. Then, taking turns, the remaining groups either endorse or dispute the choices of the presenting group. Afterwards, the correct version of the passage is presented to all groups and, for each correctly filled in gap, a point is awarded. The group with most points wins.

v. Filling blanks

Purpose and Aims

To promote debate through close reading. The activity encourages a deeper understanding of texts, beginning at the level of lexis.

Accessories

Word cards, excerpts from a text, question cards, a board and dice optional.

Process

This game may be played either in groups or pairs. The students are given either a number of extracts from a given text or one longer quotation. These will have missing words which they have to fill in. To help them with the task, they are also given a list of potential words. This list, however, may contain rogue words. Their first task is to read the text and fill in the words. This part should test their knowledge of the text as well as generate some debate. After they've completed this part, they're given a general question in relation to a particular text. For example, in relation to Dickens and *Great Expectations*, the question could be: 'Is Dickens a feminist or pro-gender equality?' They are then required to prepare a response either pro or against – the choice is theirs. Their response, however, will have to draw upon the extract or extracts they've been working with.

Outcomes and Reflections

Through the exposure to the other groups' presentations, the students acquire a more comprehensive understanding of the text and the issue at stake. The persuasiveness of individual arguments is then scored by the remaining groups, anonymously, i.e. they'll write the scores on pieces of paper which will be collected after each presentation. After the presentations, the correct words will be revealed and for each one guessed correctly, each group scores a point. These points are then added up with the points for presentations and the winner selected.

Variations

For a more gamely alternative, use a simple board, around which the students move collecting words. This could be a very simple board containing blank squares, word squares and, perhaps, trap squares which make progress more difficult. Since the onus of the game is on text and debate, keep the collecting stage as short as possible.

Yet another variation may involve keeping the overarching question the same for all and using different excerpts, or vice versa. This carries the added bonus of demonstrating the interpretability of texts.

vi. Scrabbling

Purpose and Aims

To introduce literary history through play.

Accessories

Small strips of card with words, blank sheets of paper, markers, dice.

Process

The game follows the principle of Scrabble and may be played in either pairs or groups. The number of players per group is of less importance, although it will have an impact on the number of strips that need to be produced. All the strips of paper are placed face down. The students begin by throwing a die to decide who is going to move first. Then, they take turns drawing a strip from the pile. Only one strip contains a complete word which begins with a capital letter, for example Modernism; the remaining strips, which include the names of associated figures, works or events, have the first letter of each word missing. The student who draws the Modernism card begins the game proper. From then on, the students take turns matching their strips to letters in the initial strip; however, as they game progresses they will be able to use the letters in all the strips already laid down. Once the students have used all the strips accumulated at the beginning, they proceed to draw them from the pile. If a student cannot find a match for her or his strip, s/he keeps it until the next turn and so on. The game continues until all the strips disappear from the pile and one of the players in each group uses all her or his strips; s/he becomes the winner of the group.

Outcomes and Reflections

The students take stock of the words matched and draw up an outline of the literary movement on the blank sheets provided, which they proceed to present to their peers. Through the exposure to the presentations, the students acquire different perspectives on the subject and naturally reflect on their own output. To maintain the spirit of play, after each presentation the tutor or an impartial judge chosen from amongst the students makes a note of the number of terms used and announces the winner – the group with the most matches.

vii. Shadows

Purpose and Aims

To promote independent thinking and conceptualisation. The centripetal approach of this game naturally fosters a deeper engagement with concepts, often abstract, the understanding of which frequently proves challenging to students. By both allowing them to draw on their existing knowledge and confront their assumptions, the game will lead them to new insights.

Accessories

Strips of card with words, A3 size sheets of paper, Blu-Tack, markers.

Process

The game requires a minimum of two players. The students in each pair or group are given a number of strips of paper with words. These should be reasonably big and clear so that they can be reused in presentations that will follow. For a lesson devoted to the concept of, for example, ideology, the supporting words may include: propaganda, freedom of speech, class, capitalism, privilege, institution, norm, law, prohibition, order, text, punishment, values, culture and so on. The students' task is to find the 'shadows' of these concepts – words, the meanings of which these terms imply, for example: order – anarchy, norm – difference, law – stricture, or freedom of speech – censorship. They write these down on the sheet provided, as the total number of words, scored at a point per word, will form part of their final score. Next, they are asked to label all the words using only one term and, on the basis of their findings, provide their own definition of the term and justify it. If a group guesses the actual term, it wins the game; the runner up is the group who identifies the most shadow words. If, however, nobody guesses the term, the teacher reveals it and the winner is decided on the basis of shadow words identified.

Outcomes and Reflections

The first stage of the game organically engenders reflection as students work through their word choices; while the second, more conceptual, stage of the game provides an opportunity for further reflection on these choices in order to agree a collective label and compose a definition. Through the presentations that follow, the groups receive additional feedback.

Variations

To reduce the element of chance in defining the umbrella term, you could introduce a clue card which will contain the word in question and related concepts, for example: society, country, ideology. To enhance the aesthetic appeal of the game, picture cards instead of word cards may be used, or, a combination of the two.

viii. Words in time

Purpose and Aims

This game encourages students to think about how words have changed their meaning over time, and how word meanings affect the interpretation of texts as well as debates about the validity of different interpretations. You might choose some old friends such as 'awful' or some less obvious ones such as 'romance'.

Accessories

A selection of (e.g.) six poems or extracts with key words deleted. Ideally you should have access to the complete Oxford English Dictionary (OED), either in print or online, but you may find alternative sources that help.

Process

Divide students into small groups. Present each group with the edited extracts and give them time to read them and start thinking about the missing words. Then, using your research in the OED, give them at least two definitions for each missing word, but without mentioning the word. Students must identify the missing word and the correct definition in each case. The first group to get there wins.

Outcomes and Reflections

You could use the OED examples to investigate whether each use was typical in its time or a little unusual. Open up a discussion about the legitimacy of different readings depending on the historical information provided by the dictionary. You could even invite the students to write a poem using all the missing words in all multiple definitions, but without stating what the definitions are.

Variations

You can open up the discussion to think about the meaning of metaphors, for example. Take a simile from Shakespeare and look for visual material from the period that represents the same thing. Present the images to the students and ask them to identify which of a number of passages from the set text they resemble. Then discuss whether the tone or manner of the passages and images seems the same.

2

Games about Character and Point of View

i. Actions and motives

Purpose and Aims

To foster close engagement with a text, beginning at the level of description and progressing to analysis. The game aids conceptualisation while consolidating knowledge.

Accessories

Cards, excerpts from a text, blank sheets of paper.

Process

Working in groups, students are given a set of cards bearing, for example, characters' names and, ideally, contradictory passages from a text pertaining to those characters. The latter can be actual descriptions, actions, motives and so on. First, they have to match the names with what they think are passages describing them. The challenge is that no character, however caricatured, is entirely one-dimensional. On a separate sheet of paper, students prepare a list of, for example, five criteria they used for their attribution.

Outcomes and Reflections

The results of this categorisation are then shared at the class level, after which the tutor poses a question to initiate debate. The complexity of the question may vary depending on the level of the students, for example: In *Enduring Love,* does Ian McEwan present Joe Rose as a successful male? How do McEwan's heroes depart from the masculine stereotype?

Variations

Try introducing passages describing characters from the author's other works. The groups get a point for every rogue excerpt they eliminate and another point for identifying which text it came from. Looking forward to the section of this book dealing with Games about Theory and Concepts, link this game to an introduction to deconstruction by encouraging students to think about what principles of difference might be used to dismantle apparent connections or resemblances between parts of a text.

ii. Boarding the question

Purpose and Aims

To stimulate conceptualisation while promoting group work and discussion. In its gradual approach, from gathering information to analysis, the game replicates and promotes understanding of research processes.

Accessories

Board, dice, thematic cards.

Process

The students begin by moving counters around a simple board that contains two kinds of squares: 'reveal' and 'bonus'. In the centre, face down, are placed cut up pieces of the overarching question. Every time a student lands on the 'reveal square', a piece of the overarching question falls into place; every time the 'bonus square' is occupied, s/he collects additional information which the group keeps. When all the pieces of the question have been revealed, the group is presented with a passage from a given text. The question will relate to this passage, for example: 'How does Fitzgerald tell the story in Chapter 1?' In this scenario, the bonus cards may contain information on narration techniques, mood, voice, perspective and so on:

Narrator:
- 'one who tells, or is assumed to be telling, the story in a given narrative'
- 'the narrator is the imagined 'voice' transmitting the story, and is distinguished both from the real author (who may have written other tales with very different narrators) and from the implied author (who does not recount the story, but is inferred as the authority responsible for selecting it and inventing a narrator for it.'

Oxford Dictionary of Literary Terms

Narrators:
- Homodiegetic – 'inside his narrative as in first-person stories'
- Heterodiegetic – 'absent from his own narrative' (omniscient)
- Autodiegetic – 'where he is not only inside the narrative but figures as its principal character'

Terry Eagleton, Literary Theory, 106.

Reliable narrators are those 'whose accounts of events we are obliged to trust'.
Unreliable narrators are those 'whose accounts may be partial, ill-informed, or misleading'.
'[M]ost third-person narrators are reliable, but some first-person narrators are unreliable.'

Oxford Dictionary of Literary Terms

The theoretical scope of the material contained in the bonus cards will need to reflect and match the complexity of the question.

The first round of the game is designed to be played dynamically, and the quicker the players finish it, the more time they'll have to discuss the passage. Each group presents their findings at the end of the game and is scored on the persuasiveness of their argument.

Outcomes and Reflections

The blend of theory and practice here encourages students to deconstruct narrative method and understand how an author's choices impact on interpretation. The closing presentations serve as feedback from the tutor and between groups.

Variations

Each group works with a different textual extract; or, groups work with a number of identical but shorter passages to answer a general question: 'Are unreliable narration and veracity mutually exclusive?; or, 'Does Fitzgerald's *The Great Gatsby* challenge the notion of objectivity? If so, how?'

iii. Rewriting

Purpose and Aims

To encourage students to think in terms of cause and effect and their combined impact on the structure and the telling of narrative. The game stimulates creativity and promotes close textual engagement.

Accessories

Extracts from the set text; timer.

Process

Each group of students is given a different passage from a particular text. First, they have to identify who speaks in the passage or narrates it (you can time this part and award points); second, they have to present it from another character's perspective; and third, list the implications for the whole narrative in terms of plot and structure if it were written from that character's perspective: which aspects of the plot would be emphasised and which downplayed, what would be revealed and what concealed and so on. Before proceeding to task two and three, and after the identification round, the groups are awarded a point for each correctly named character. The game concludes with a round of presentations of alternative narratives, which are scored anonymously. The combined score of the first round and the presentation round (and the timed section if you decide to use it) decides the winner.

Outcomes and Reflections

Playing with narrative helps the students understand the notion of causality and plausibility, all the while fostering a deeper engagement with a given text.

Variations

All groups work with the same passage. The results may be interesting. To simplify matters, the students are told from whose perspective they are to present the narrative. You could use the game to help students put the concept of defamiliarisation into practice. To make the task more challenging, add a stipulation that while they may change any linguistic aspect of the narrative, they may not change the chronology of events. By way of feedback, the students read out their pieces to the other groups and explain the rationale behind their choices, for example what aspects of the excerpts and language they focused on and why. The presentations are scored anonymously and the winner selected.

Another attempt at defamiliarisation may involve the students changing a part of the plot. In this scenario, a representative of each group draws a card with instructions as to which aspect of the narrative they are to alter without undermining the plausibility of the narrative as a whole. They present the result to the remaining groups, explaining why such a revision is justifiable and plausible. The most persuasive argument wins. The game would not only promote a deeper engagement with a given text, but also, implicitly, convey the idea of the constructedness of every narrative. A slight twist of the game would involve all groups working with the same aspect of the plot, but unbeknownst to one another.

iv. Characters and concepts

Purpose and Aims

To enhance students' analytical skills through examination of the relationship between the development of characters and the evolution of concepts. The activity promotes confidence in formulating and justifying arguments while fostering a deeper understanding of a text.

Accessories

Textual excerpts, narrative map, a sheet of A3 paper, marker pens.

Process

The students are presented with fragments of a given text which they are asked to arrange in order. These excerpts should be judiciously selected to reflect the development of the concept, such as gender, class, race, or identity, its different conceptions held by characters and so on. First, the players attempt to connect the excerpts with the turning points or events from a given narrative. Those turning points need to be pre-described on a simple chart. Students pin the excerpts to the chart. For every correct identification, the group earns a point. Next, they arrange them in a way that best demonstrates the evolution of the concept and they have to justify the chosen order. Then, they compare the development of the concept with the development of the narrative, the key points of which they have already sketched, to see if they can detect a pattern, similarities or differences. The activity ends with groups presenting their findings. The group who identifies the most, wins.

Outcomes and Reflections

After the presentations, initiate a discussion by posing a question, for example: 'What would be the implications if the author structured the text differently?' The question allows the students to reflect upon the interdependence between the constructedness of narrative and evolution of concepts, thus consolidating their newly acquired knowledge.

Variations

The activity proceeds as above, but this time the students' task is to scrutinise the development of a character. They present their findings to the other groups and are scored anonymously. At the end of the lesson, the scores are compared and the winner selected.

v. Other shoes

Purpose and Aims

To build confidence in presenting arguments in the relative safety of the circle of play. This role-playing game tests the students' knowledge of a given text and provides insights into creative process while stimulating debate. This is a version of a game often used in teaching drama.

Accessories

Cards, a sheet of paper, marker pens.

Process

Working in groups, students choose a representative. S/he
approaches a table and is told to take two sets of cards, one green
and the other red. S/he keeps the red ones and distributes the
green ones among the group. The cards contain the students' new
identities either as a character (green cards), or an author (red card).
Unbeknownst to the representative, s/he has become the author. The
character cards may list potential grievances and questions they as
characters may wish to ask the author. The author cards will suggest
potential responses, referring perhaps to the rationale behind the
plot and character construction. Characters may reproach their
authors for constructing them in the way they did, while authors are
forced to defend their positions. Depending on the context, the cards
might contain a broad spectrum of information which the authors
would draw upon in their defence. The character cards could contain
suggestions about ideal ways in which they think they should be
written. Ensuing discussion typically follows an argument-counter
argument pattern and promotes contextualising, extending to
include concepts of potential readers. The authors and characters are
ultimately required to reach a consensus and justify it to the rest of
the class, so representing the process of compromise and elimination
by which texts come into being.

Outcomes and Reflections

Although seemingly easy, the game demands a thorough knowledge
of a given text. Looking through a character's eyes enables students
to confront the narrative and ideological decisions made, consciously
or otherwise, in the process of writing. It also challenges them
to decide whether it is possible to identify with a character, thus
questioning the most commonly accepted reason why people
like or dislike certain books, and see that the possibility of one
interpretation is unsustainable, even from 'within' the work.

Variations

Looking ahead again to Theory and Concepts, you could try this. Instead of the author and character cards, students assume the roles of theorists and 'students'. The theorist cards contain the precepts of a particular theory and the reasons why it should be applied to interpretation. The student cards, on the other hand, point to potential gaps in the theory and the way it may prove to be insufficient to interpretation of certain texts. To increase the range of the game, the student cards may carry examples of texts with which they confront the author and ask him to demonstrate how the theory would work.

There is further scope for variation possible here, for example: all the student cards in each group deal with different aspects of one text. Therefore, if there are four groups in the class, the theory may be tested on four different works and probed to a reasonable depth. At the end of the game, each group presents their findings to the other groups. These may include areas of consensus reached between theorists and students in each group as well as points of difference.

Yet another version of the game may be used as a revision exercise at the end of the semester, whereby each group deals with a different theoretical problem. The debates that follow act as debriefing for the observers.

vi. Shifting viewpoints

Purpose and Aims

To help the students to explore the multi-layered nature of narrative. The game builds the students' confidence in working closely with texts and formulating hypotheses. It promotes a critical and selective approach to text.

Accessories

Excerpts, task cards, blank sheets of paper.

Process

Imagine that instead of an existing narrator, the story is put into somebody else's hands. The students work in groups or pairs and are given strips with key events and turning points in the narrative and a task card to be looked at after the first activity has been completed. Alternatively, the task cards could be distributed after the first part of the exercise has been completed. The task cards will require them to present a version of the narrative from a particular character's perspective and discuss the potential of the re-write for the drift of the narrative. First, they proceed to put these in chronological order, for which they may be awarded points. Second, they present the story from a particular character's perception. In order to do so, they will need to analyse a particular character first and then decide which aspects of the narrative will have to be emphasised and which downplayed or omitted altogether. As usual, they'll present the re-writes to the rest of the class, including the rationale behind the composition. Points are awarded anonymously, based on persuasiveness.

Outcomes and Reflections

Moving from character to the bigger picture, the game encourages students to reflect on the constructedness of narrative and its impact on meaning. After the presentations, ask each group to list three things they have learned about the narrative by re-writing a part of it.

vii. Characters and places

Purpose and Aims

To facilitate the understanding of concepts such as marginality and centrality. The game aims to promote group work and discussion, and build the students' confidence in constructing arguments.

Accessories

Excerpts, blank sheets of paper, question cards.

Process

Divided into groups, students are presented with fragments of texts that describe different settings. For each place, they have to come up with a number of adjectives that best define it. For example, when talking of Gatsby's residence, these could range from big, imposing, rich, opulent, magnificent, secluded, crowded, gaudy, overstated and so on. Once this has been completed, they set out to explore whether the inhabitants of these places may be described using the same adjectives. They may either be given a certain number of characters to discuss, for example four, or the choice may be left to them. What they are looking for are correspondences or differences between the places and the characters dwelling within their walls. Each group is then given a different question to answer, for example: What causes characters to be out of place if the same adjectives can be used to describe them? Can place make a character central even if his characteristics point to marginality? Is marginality a matter of place? To even out the playing field and preserve the spirit of the game, each group, before it commences the presentation, states the number of adjectives they have used to describe the place and is awarded a point for each. The teacher, as a scorekeeper, makes a note of the scores. The groups proceed to present their findings to the rest of the groups and are scored anonymously. The combined score for the two rounds decides the winner.

Outcomes and Reflections

The presentations provide feedback to the groups. Since they work with different though related questions, the students gain a more comprehensive understanding of the issue at stake while broadening their knowledge of the text or texts discussed.

Variations

All groups engage with an identical question. This is more intense but encourages specific debate about an assessment question you may choose to introduce.

viii. Who's Talking?

Purpose and Aims

To reveal the subtext of a text through close reading. The activity focuses on exploring the differences between the characters' own perceptions of themselves and other characters' descriptions of them or their actions. For example, working with Sebastian Barry's *The Secret Scripture*, the exercise could focus on Roseanne's or the narrator's descriptions of her and the perceptions of other characters such as Dr Grene. As such, it facilitates a more comprehensive understanding of a text.

Accessories

Excerpts from a text, blank sheets of paper.

Process

The students, divided into pairs, are presented with a number of excerpts from a given text and, first, they have to attribute them to one of the characters. Then they focus on words and phrases that imply value judgements – any words that may reveal something of either the speaker or the object. They are asked to make a list of these words and justify their selection. Having looked at opposing descriptions of, for example, Roseanne, they are then faced with a question: 'Is Roseanne's illness real or imagined?; What does the text reveal about society?' Now they have to work with the words but 'against' the text to re-construct the picture of Roseanne. Scoring is divided into two parts: the matching round whereby the groups are awarded a point for each correctly identified excerpt; and the presentation round which is scored anonymously. The scores from the two rounds are added at the end and the winner proclaimed. Collecting points as play unfolds adds dynamism to the game and increases competition which is an integral part of the idea of a game.

Outcomes and Reflections

They present the portraits to the rest of the groups and answer the question or questions posed. The most convincing presentation wins. Effectively, through reading against the grain, the students uncover the values underpinning character construction.

Variations

This type of game of reading against the grain could be adapted to any text and virtually any scenario. Try slipping in a rogue passage from another book by the same author. See if students identify it and when the secret is out discuss the similarities and differences.

ix. Conflict

Purpose and Aims

To explore the subtext of a text. The game rests on the assumption that there's no literature without 'conflict, or love, or both together', as Huizinga puts it, and aims to promote a deeper understanding of the text as well as provoke critical reflection. It encourages the students to explore latent conflicts existing between the characters' desires and actions.

Accessories

A board, cards, blank sheets of paper, marker pens.

Process

The game requires a simple board with colour-coded squares corresponding to card categories: characters' names, actions, and excerpts from the text describing their desires. The collecting round will either last for a given amount of time or long enough to allow the players to collect a certain amount of cards in each category. The students' first task is to match characters with their desires and actions. Now, they begin to examine what the characters want to do and what they actually do and identify the reasons governing their behaviour. They produce a list of their findings.

Outcomes and Reflections

They present their findings to the other groups, and the group who identifies the most conflicts wins. Now, initiate discussion on the veracity of the statement that love, conflict or both underpin all literary production. The answers you receive are likely to reach beyond the perimeter of the game.

x. Negation

Purpose and Aims

To promote understanding of a text, its mechanics, construction of narrative and the ways in which they combine to influence readers' interpretations. Through the construction of an alternative narrative, the game aims at fostering a deeper understanding of a text and encourages critical reflection.

Accessories

A board, cards, blank sheets of paper.

Process

The game utilises a simple board with colour-coded squares corresponding to two card categories: events and characters. These mix and match events and character traits from the narrative and attribute them to other characters. An example from *Pride and Prejudice* may include the following cards: the Bennetts are rich, Darcy is poor, Lydia is virtuous, Mary is frivolous, Kitty is wise, Bingley marries Georgiana, Lizzy marries Wickham, Jane becomes an old maid and so on. Students move around the board, collecting events and then they arrange them in order (the fictional events should transform the narrative but not its linearity). Then they draw up a list of actual events corresponding to the alternative ones, and are awarded a point for every correctly identified pair. Then, they are presented with a question: 'Why doesn't the narrative follow the alternative path?'

Outcomes and Reflections

The question forces them to consider the implications of the plot and character on interpretation. The groups present their findings to the other groups and are scored on persuasiveness.

Variations

The activity is easily adaptable to discussions of diverse topics depending on the objective of the lesson.

3

Games about Texts and Contexts

i. Context basics

Purpose and Aims

To facilitate contextualising and application of newly gained knowledge to the analysis of texts. The game builds the students' confidence in constructing arguments, helps them to consolidate knowledge of a text and tests their understanding of its period of composition.

Accessories

A simple board (Ludo-style), a die, a sheet of paper, marker pens.

Process

Use a simple board and cards. The information on the cards should be specific, and the questions asked could vary in format from general yes or no questions (*Pride and Prejudice* was written after the Battle of Waterloo, etc) to multiple-choice options (the defeated French leader at Waterloo was called (a) Louis XVI, (b) Louis Philippe, (c) Robespierre (d) Napoleon). Each student in the group rolls a die and the one with the highest score begins the game. The student rolls a die, moves her/his counter and, when s/he lands on a question square, the next student picks up a card and asks her/him a question. If s/he answers the question correctly, s/he keeps the card. The student who collects the most cards wins this round. This round should be timed by the teacher or a designated student and shouldn't last longer than 10 minutes. The group then takes stock of the cards they have collected and proceeds to list on a sheet of paper provided what they consider to be the characteristics of the period. Following this, they are asked a simple task, for example: 'Identify the ways in which *Pride and Prejudice* reflects and/or resists its times'.

Outcomes and Reflections

Each group presents their findings at class forum and the presentations are scored anonymously. The game marks a foray into historicist examination of cohesive patterns or dissonances between texts and their historical and cultural contexts. If time permits, initiate a discussion about whether the dissonances are more important than the cohesive patterns. As has often been observed, the idea that everyone in a given period thought the same way is disproved whenever you open a history book and find them killing each other because they couldn't agree…

Variations

To save time, try dispensing with the board and limit the students to drawing cards and answering questions. Introduce rogue cards containing incorrect information which the students have to identify and exclude from the profile of the period. For every incorrect piece of information that makes its way into the final presentation, a point is deducted. You could move beyond information and include samples of texts from other periods.

ii. Context building

Purpose and Aims

To foster understanding of the interdependence between literary text and historical context. The game enhances the students' analytical abilities by encouraging them to look beyond the text.

Accessories

Cards, a sheet of paper, marker pens.

Process

Students working in groups are given cards with fragments of historical texts, travel narratives, literary texts and pictures. First, they have to match a picture with a thematically corresponding historical text. At the end of the exercise, they are given the right order. This part of the game adopts a chronological approach to demonstrate how a concept was constructed and evolved over time. Next, the students are presented with excerpts from a specific literary text and a simple question, for example: 'Discuss whether *Huck Finn* depends upon or challenges assumptions about racial identity?' As in previous examples, the players present their findings to the groups and are scored anonymously.

Outcomes and Reflections

The presentations allow the students to reflect upon historically and socially charged concepts such as, for example, race or alterity. As part of the debriefing stage, and after the presentations, ask them to list, say five, common misconceptions about the concept under discussion.

Variations

As an exercise in research skill, ask students (a week ahead) to find examples that they will feed into the game. You could even challenge them to see if they can test your own knowledge, if you're feeling courageous.

iii. Context testing

Purpose and Aims

To aid argument building. The game tests students' knowledge of a given text. It encourages critical thinking through the process of distillation of material.

Accessories

Excerpts from texts, quotation cards.

Process

It's based on a question that can be as simply or sophisticatedly phrased as the level requires (e.g. 'Was Shakespeare a royalist?'). Take up to fifteen quotation cards, all about kingship. Eight (for example) are from the play, and the rest from other Shakespeare plays. The first task is to identify the ones from *Macbeth* – simple case of who gets the most right first. Then, the tutor introduces further quotation cards. One set has some contemporary material about the divine right of kings (try James I's 1610 speech to Parliament); the other, explanations of the relationship between that material and the plays. The students have to take the non-*Macbeth* quotations first and choose which explanation cards offer the most convincing case. Then they move to the *Macbeth* ones and do the same.

Outcomes and Reflections

Now, they move to a discussion of the original question but nuanced to take account of the differences between *Macbeth* and the other extracts.

Variations

To take the level of difficulty up a notch, introduce additional points for identifying the relevant stage of the play, not just the title. Use some iconography of kingship from the period for further variety.

iv. More context testing

Purpose and Aims

To foster a deeper engagement with a text within a specific context. The tiered design of the game promotes the extrapolation of interpretation from word level to the text as a whole, fostering comparison and debate.

Accessories

Textual extracts, envelopes, crib sheets.

Process:

This game starts by posing a reasonably challenging question about the relationship between a given text and an aspect of its historical context. For the sake of demonstration, the text chosen is Marlowe's *Doctor Faustus,* but it would be possible to base versions of the game on any number of prose, poetic and dramatic narratives.

The question posed to students at the outset is 'Evaluate the relationship between *Doctor Faustus* and Calvinist narratives of sin'. Take 15 extracts from the play (all of them of Faustus himself talking) and cut them into cards. Jumble each set in an envelope. Students work in pairs or threes (could be more) to put them in the right order.

This is partly a test of their knowledge of the play but encourages them to think about a variety of ways of making sense of Faustus's self-narrative. Move round and talk to them as they do this but remind them they are working against the clock. After 10-15 minutes ask them to stop and discuss their decisions in a plenary. Take an example of theological literature (William Perkins on the progress of sin is a good choice), consider its narrative and then return to the Faustus extracts, asking students to review in pairs/threes their initial order in the light of the Perkins extract. Stop for a plenary discussion of the changes they have made, if any, and why they are significant. Give them a crib sheet with the correct order of the *Faustus* extracts (depending on how competitive you want to be, name the winning group), and ask them to discuss in pairs/threes the extent to which the play maps onto the Perkins extract. There's endless room for argument: it does and it doesn't, and what tends to be revealed is the ambiguity and complexity of the literary text in relation to the context.

Bring everyone back for a plenary and ask them to discuss – without tutor input – the question given at the top of this task sheet. Allow 10-15 minutes. Tutor concludes, reviewing general points about the fractured, unpredictable nature of the relationship between text and the theological context, and looking at key examples of where Faustus narrates his destiny to us. Whose is this narrative voice, really? What ideological conditions shape it, or don't? After a break, review and move on to longer passages/themes in a more conventional seminar format. By now, students have had practical experience of looking closely at theme and voice in the extracts.

Outcomes and Reflections

You could object that this gives students a partial view of the play. Care has to be shown in making the initial selection of extracts. They need to be short to make the exercise efficient, but of course any seminar session is selective to some degree, and an advantage of this approach is that it is geared towards a long trajectory, a whole reading. Another advantage is that the exercise takes a demanding central theme, strongly related to bigger methodological questions about how to read literature in context, which is nonetheless grounded in manageable chunks. The students look at those chunks often enough to start remembering them and it is invariably possible to see phrases and ideas sinking in as they complete the exercise. When they go back to reading the whole play, the extracts function as landmarks to give them a greater sense of familiarity.

v. Contextual reasoning

Purpose and Aims

To contextualise a particular text, thus building analytical skills and aiding interpretation. To this end, the game will allow the students to draw upon sources and extract information to build a picture of the historical and biographical context in which a text is created.

Accessories

Cards, a board, counters, dice, a blank sheet of paper for designing a poster, marker pens, Blu-Tack etc.

Process

This game calls for a more active involvement on the part of the teacher who acts as a facilitator. The colours of card categories correspond to the squares on the board, and may include dates, historical information, biographical information on the author and, if possible, quotations from the text relating to the aforementioned, particularly in relation to historical information. For a seminar focused on F. Scott Fitzgerald's *The Great Gatsby* and the depictions of the lower social classes as 'crude and vulgar' (a topic borrowed from the AQA A-Level syllabus), the following card categories may be useful: dates, historical facts, including information on the author, and quotations.

1865

The U.S. Congress ratifies the Thirteenth Amendment to the Constitution prohibiting slavery

1896

Racial segregation begins in the South

1919

Prohibition of the manufacture and sale of alcohol
Women are granted the right to vote

1896

The birth of F. Scott Fitzgerald

'It had occurred to me that this shadow of a garage must be a blind and that sumptuous and romantic apartments were concealed overhead when the proprietor himself appeared in the door of an office, wiping his hands on a piece of waste. He was a blonde, spiritless man, anaemic, and faintly handsome.'
F. Scott Fitzgerald,
The Great Gatsby, 28.

'The friends looked out at us with the tragic eyes and short upper lips of south-eastern Europe, and I was glad that the sight of Gatsby's splendid car was included in their sombre holiday. As we crossed Blackwell's Island a limousine passed us driven by a white chauffeur, in which sat three modish Negroes, two bucks and a girl. I laughed aloud as the yolks of their eyeballs rolled toward us in a haughty rivalry.'
F. Scott Fitzgerald,
The Great Gatsby, 74.

Students throw the dice and move around the board collecting cards. This part of the game may either be timed, for example, 10 minutes; or, as above, it ends as soon as a group completes a set. The students' first task will be to look at the cards and arrange them in order, matching dates with events etc. They exclude quotation cards from this timeline. After this has been accomplished, the actual order of events is given, and each group earns a point for every correctly matched event and date. They are then given a minute to rearrange their timeline accordingly, and move to the second stage of the game. At the centre of the board, and at the beginning of the game, the teacher places a card containing a question, face down. Only after the first stage of the game has been completed are the students allowed to look at the card. This question will be text specific and formulated in such a way that allows the students to draw connections or observe differences between the information collected on cards and the text; to demonstrate the dialogic relationship between the text and context, and to discuss it. They present the conclusions on the blank sheet of paper. The posters are scored separately, and the combined scores of the poster and timeline rounds decide the winner.

Outcomes and Reflections

In checking the accuracy of their timelines, the students receive instant feedback during play, which allows them to correct their errors. The feedback received after each presentation and the exposure to the work of their peers will further broaden their understanding of the text as well as emphasise the interdependence between text and context, whether it be symbiotic or antagonistic.

Variations

To demonstrate the malleability of interpretation while allowing for a more comprehensive engagement with the text, devise a different question for each group. The accessories could be made text, subject specific or kept at a general level so that they can be reapplied to different scenarios. Alternatively, there could be sufficient number of cards designed at the outset to allow for some to be removed or added to meet the demands of different scenarios. For example, variations of this game could be designed to teach about genres or language as well as abstract concepts such as difference, race, grotesque, centrality and marginality.

vi. Writing summaries

Purpose and Aims

To promote a closer engagement with a text, both at the analytical and lexical levels. The game allows the students to practise their interpretative and writing skills.

Accessories

Passages from a text, blank sheets of paper, markers.

Process

Working in groups, each student is given a passage from a given text with the stipulation that they cannot show it to one another. Their task is to summarise the text in a set amount of words. They are not allowed to use any strategic words that may give the game away, for example proper names. Once they have produced their summaries, each student reads hers/his aloud, and collectively they decide in what order they should be arranged. Next, they reveal the textual fragments they have summarised, arrange them in order, and compare the two narratives. The tutor then reveals the correct order of the actual excerpts, and for every correctly matched pair, each group is awarded a point. More important, however, are those excerpts which have not been matched, and the students turn to those now. Their task is to scrutinise both and come up with plausible reasons why the order changed and what implications such change may have for the narrative as a whole. They are asked to prepare a list of these, dividing them into two categories: cause and effect. The group that comes up with the most receives the highest number of points, which are then added to the points earned during the first round. The combined score decides the winner.

Outcomes and Reflections

The game allows the students to reflect on lexical choices and consider their implications for narrative and interpretation. These elements of analysis are more often than not overlooked by students who tend to focus on plot and action.

vii. Challenging stereotypes

Purpose and Aim

To examine how literary texts endorse or challenge stereotypes. The activity allows the students to practice their analytical skills and promotes close engagement with literary texts.

Accessories

Cards, textual excerpts, a sheet of A3 paper, marker pens.

Process

Working in groups, students are presented with excerpts from contemporary texts describing, for example, femininity. These could come from an array of sources including theoretical texts and popular media. Their first task is to draft a modern conception of femininity and decide what societal expectations support it. They may list individual characteristics in bullet points. Next, they are given a profile of a female character, for example Catherine Earnshaw in *Wuthering Heights,* composed from excerpts taken from the text and headed with a question: 'Cathy Earnshaw: a feminine woman or a woman ahead of her time?'; or 'Femininity: fact or enduring fiction?' They compile another list of the societal expectations that influence or bear on Cathy. Finally, they identify the parallels and differences between the conceptions of femininity now and then and present their conclusions to the class.

Outcomes and Reflections

Looking for parallels and differences between the two will force the students to question stereotypes and see constructions like femininity as context specific. It will also enable them to confront their own assumptions, whether they be socially or culturally informed.

viii. Pursuing trivia

Purpose and Aims

To challenge or endorse assumptions and facilitate an inter-textual and centripetal approach to narrative and interpretation. This game promotes an in-depth engagement with literary texts and critical thinking.

Accessories

Thematic cards, record sheets, task cards, blank sheets of paper, marker pens.

Process

Working in groups, students are presented with a set of thematic cards containing, for example, descriptions of places from a particular text or a number of texts, for example Angela Carter's collection *The Bloody Chamber:*

'The faery solitude of the place;
with its turrets of misty blue,
its courtyard, its spiked gate,
his castle that lay on the very
bosom of the sea with seabirds
mewing about its attics... that
castle, at home neither on
the land nor on the water, a
mysterious, amphibious place,
contravening the materiality of
both earth and the waves, with
the melancholy of a mermaiden
who perches on her rock and
waits, endlessly, for a lover who
had drowned far away, long
ago. That lovely, sad, sea-siren
of a place.'

They take turns selecting cards and guessing answers: given the place description they have to guess the name of character that dwells there and come up with a number of words or phrases that describe the character and place. They record the results of their task on a character/place sheet provided. Ideally, the students will have obtained an overview of class distinctions, which then will be used to compare or include new characters. Next, they are presented with a problem statement: 'Whether intentionally or not, all novels are about class – discuss in relation to.....'

Next, to test the assumption, they transfer the characteristics they have identified in the first part of the game to the characters and their dwellings of the text under scrutiny and each group demonstrates its findings to the rest of the class. They are likely to find many correspondences.

Outcomes and Reflections

Working at the level of language, the students have a chance to observe for themselves how literary conceptions of class are constructed through language. Round up the presentations by posing yet another question, for example: 'Do places influence the language we use? If so, why?'

Variations

This type of a game that opens with a potentially contentious statement may be adapted to a number of scenarios such as plot construction, character construction, oppositions, marginality, to name just a few.

ix. What if this…

Purpose and Aims

To explore a text's unconscious. This is a board game which aims at exploring socio-cultural values underpinning the composition of texts. It fosters debate and invites the students to question the artifice of narrative.

Accessories

A simple board, dice, blank sheets of paper, markers.

Process

The game may be played in pairs or groups and utilises a simple board. The students throw a die and move around the board, on which there are squares asking them to conjure up alternative scenarios. These could be quite general: alternative hero/heroine, major event, turning point, a scandal, setting and so on. They jot down their ideas as they go along. Then, they take some time to weave those into a story outline and, lastly, compare the alternative story with the actual one.

Outcomes and Reflections

Following this, they present to the remaining groups the alternative story and the reasons why such ending wasn't possible for the author. The presentations are scored on their persuasiveness.

Variations

Before they proceed to write an alternative scenario, each group receives a card listing the characters who must be included in the re-telling. Another variation of this game could include moving around the board as above but, instead of conjuring up alternative scenarios, the students are firstly required to deal with actual events which they write down. Once this has been completed, they construct an opposite version of each event and end up weaving an alternative narrative. Again, the game may be made as flexible or specific as the objective of the lesson requires.

x. What if that…

Purpose and Aims

To explore a text's unconscious through an examination of the socio-cultural values that inform it and the other texts that lie behind it. It naturally promotes discussion and creativity without losing sight of criticism and theory.

Accessories

Cards, blank sheets of paper, markers.

Process

The first stage of the game is based on an old children's card game called 'Peter'. It's very simple, consisting of twelve pairs of cards identifying actual events from the text (Othello smothers Desdemona) and alternative scenarios (he forgives her but kills himself instead) and a wild card – Peter. The cards are dealt and the players take turns drawing the cards from one another. The aim of the game is to pair as many as possible. The loser is left with the Peter card, which invites the players to elaborate an alternative story including suggestions from the cards. The loser becomes the clerk responsible for keeping a record of the group's proceedings.

Outcomes and Reflections

Throughout the creative part, the students are forced to confront the actual story with their alternative, thus consolidating their knowledge of a text. The presentations should explain what, in terms of the message of the original text, the alternative version questions or challenges. As usual, they are scored on the persuasiveness of their arguments.

Variations

The game provides a neat way of dealing with stories that already exist in different versions, like *King Lear* or *The Bloody Chamber*. Try juxtaposing extracts from the different versions on paired cards and using the Peter principle to tease out further variations and so interrogate the choices made by the reviser.

xi. Walk the line

Purpose and Aims

To consolidate knowledge of a text and its historical and cultural background. Since the game is played in pairs or groups, it naturally encourages discussion and argument building.

Accessories

Cards, blank sheets of paper, markers, timer.

Process

Each pair or group is given an array of quotations from the literary text under discussion, and from historical texts, dates, pictures and so on. Students must find the connection and identify key themes such as gentility, manners, oppression of women and so on. Do this to time. The group with the highest number of valid connections wins.

Outcomes and Reflections

Students present their findings to the other groups, explaining their reasoning. In tracing connections, the students inadvertently solidify their knowledge and are encouraged to think flexibly about the relationship of text to context.

Variations

To make the activity more challenging, rogue cards may be included which the students will have to eliminate, explaining the rationale behind their decision to do so. A rogue card may contain an extract from another literary or historical text, either from the same period or another. Instead of establishing a single causal link, the students are encouraged to find as many connections as they can. Of course, they'll have to prove to the rest of the groups why the connections are justifiable.

xii. Three wishes

Purpose and Aims

To promote analytical skills and a deeper engagement with a text. The game invites the students to consider the implication of alternative outcomes on the interpretation of the text.

Accessories

A board, a die, cards.

Process

Taking turns, students move pieces around a simple board collecting cards in different categories such as characters, plot, settings, events, outcomes and so on. In the centre of the board is placed another card, face down, that contains instructions. The students may only look at that card once they've collected (for example) two or three cards in each category. Once unveiled, the card informs the students that they now have three wishes which allow them to change any parts of the narrative they choose or re-situate it in one of a number of named historical periods (so, what would change if you set *Romeo and Juliet* in modern Birmingham?). They may apply the wishes to one category or two, but have to consider the implications of the changes for the narrative as a whole: 'What would be revealed if their wishes were granted? What would be lost?' 'Why are those wishes currently frustrated?' etc.

Outcomes and Reflections

The game in itself encourages reflection as the students consider which parts of the narrative to change and the implications of such changes. The questions invite them to look beyond the text and consider socio-cultural values that underpin it. The game concludes with presentations which are scored anonymously.

xiii. Fallibility

Purpose and Aims

To promote a deeper understanding of a text by placing it within its socio-cultural context. The game illustrates the disparity between ideality and actuality, and encourages the students to look critically at the codes governing society.

Accessories

Cards, excerpts, blank sheets of paper.

Purpose

The game is loosely based on the idea of a puzzle, whereby the students, working in pairs or groups, are given a selection of words, phrases, sentences etc., describing a particular character or two. These are taken from the text and constitute 'the real'. Additionally, they're given excerpts from contemporaneous etiquette or conduct books which would denote 'the ideal'. Here's an example from Bram Stoker's *Dracula* and Florence Hartley's *The Ladies' Book of Etiquette and Manual of Politeness:*

[Mina] 'I have been working very hard lately, because I want to keep up with Jonathan's studies, and I have been practising shorthand very assiduously. When we are married I shall be able to be useful to Jonathan, and if I can stenograph well enough I can take down what he wants to say in this way and write it out for him on the typewriter, at which also I am practising very hard.'

Bram Stoker, *Dracula*, 79.

'A lady without her piano, or her pencil, her library of French, German, or Italian authors, her fancy work and her embroideries, is now rarely met with, and it is right that such arts should be universal. No woman is fitted for society until she dances well; for home, until she is a perfect mistress of needlework; for her own enjoyment, unless she has at least accomplishment to occupy thoughts and fingers in her hours of leisure.'

Florence Hartley, *The Ladies' Book of Etiquette*, 179.

Included in the array of cards are two headings: real and ideal. First, they decide which card goes under which heading. Then, they're asked a simple question: 'Does Mina Murray fit the criteria of an accomplished woman?' Their next task is to manipulate the image to arrive at the ideal.

Outcomes and Reflections

They prepare a presentation of their ideal constructions to the other groups, including a commentary on what they changed and why. The presentations are scored anonymously and the winner selected.

Variations

To gain a more contextually comprehensive view of a given text, design a set of different cards for each group so that, for example, one group examines femininity and another masculinity. The game may be played using a simple board that contains two 'must collect' squares and a number of 'collect a card' ones. The 'must collect' squares contain the headings 'real' and 'ideal'. The aim of this round would be to collect the two headings and as many cards as possible. This would necessitate some strategic planning. Only once the heading cards have been collected may the players look at the centre of the board containing the key question.

xiv. Prescriptions and proscriptions

Purpose and Aims

To enable the students to look beyond plot to examine how a text promotes rituals, social codes, gender roles and so on. The game promotes critical thinking and argument building, all through looking at circumstantial evidence.

Accessories

A board, a die, cards.

Process

The students play with a simple board, moving pieces around it and collecting cards. Depending on the objective of the lesson, these may include definitions of, for example, class, excerpts from a text and clue cards pointing the way to how the excerpts should be approached. The clue cards should communicate clearly what the students need to examine, for instance: language, characters, setting etc. The excerpts should be chosen judiciously to offer enough scope for the exploration of the clues and may contain social situations, thus enabling the students to observe both the language used and characters' position and behaviour towards one another. Before they begin to examine the cards, they are given a question or questions, for example: 'What hierarchies obtain in *Digging to America?* How are they manifested?'

Outcomes and Reflections

Through a close examination of the excerpts the students develop a deeper understanding of the text. The question posed at the end of the card-collecting round invites them to engage with the material critically, to look beyond the explicit and build a persuasive argument.

Variations

Instead of working with a number of shorter excerpts, provide a longer, different passage for each group.

4

Games about Theory and Concepts

i. Who knows?

Purpose and Aims

To consolidate knowledge and draw upon it to build new arguments. This game lends itself easily to discussions of theoretical topics as well as specific texts, and derives elements from the popular game, *Taboo.*

Accessories

A simple board, dice, concept cards and an overarching question cut up and placed in the centre.

Process

Begin by dividing your class into small groups. In each group a student draws a concept card from a pile and has to explain its content to his teammates, its purport, without using any words already on the card. If they guess correctly, the student rolls a die and moves forward. If nobody guesses, the card either goes back to the bottom of the deck, or another student may step in. The student whose explanation fails to elicit the correct response sits the round out. For every successful explanation, the student keeps the card, scores a point and a piece of the overarching question is revealed. Here are some ideas for cards that may be utilised in a session concerned with the exploration of how Dickens creates and uses suspense in *Great Expectations,* a question borrowed from AQA A-Level syllabus. Depending on whether the students are to provide the definition of a term or guess its name, the cards may contain answers and words in bold type.

Suspense – a 'temporary cessation, intermission, abeyance.'

OED

Novel
Answer: usually 'an extended fictional prose narrative'.

Oxford Dictionary
of Literary Terms

Plot
Answer: 'the pattern of events and situations in a narrative or dramatic work'.

Oxford Dictionary
of Literary Terms

Novels generate suspense by **withholding information** from the reader.

This round of the game continues until all the students in each group have crossed the finishing line. Alternatively, and to allow the students more time for composing answers, the round may stop when the first player in each group reaches the finish. From then on, the groups focus on producing an answer to the question, which they will eventually present to their peers. It is important that both the overarching question and the contents of the concept cards are thematically linked.

Outcomes and Reflections

The more ludic first stage of the game serves as a refresher for knowledge already acquired, one that encourages conceptualisation, and provides instantaneous feedback. The second stage of the game takes conceptualisation a step further by allowing the students to work with new material while applying the knowledge just recalled.

Variations

To facilitate a more detailed engagement with a text, cut up a passage into pieces, one of which will include the overarching question. The round stops when they have collected all the pieces. Before they can attempt to answer the question, the students will need to arrange the passage in order. Other possibilities include working with different passages of the same text but identical overarching questions or vice versa. Each alternative version allows for a more rounded analysis of the text in a relatively short space of time.

ii. Defining race

Purpose and Aims

To promote interpretative skills through close and critical engagement with text. The game aids building confidence, encourages independent thought and formulation of arguments.

Accessories

Cards, a simple board, counters, a die, a blank sheet of paper for designing a poster, marker pens, Blu-Tack etc.

Process

Students work in small groups, take turns rolling the dice and moving around the board collecting cards. This time, they only contend with two card categories which are distinguishable by their colours that match the squares on the board. Because the aim of this game is to let students formulate their own definitions of race, the first category of cards contains others' definitions of race and/or quotations, which have missing words. The second category of cards contains only the missing words. Here are some examples:

'To assume, by intention or default, that race is a phenomenon outside history is to take up a position within the terrain of racialist ideology and to become its unknowing – and therefore uncontesting – victim. The first move in this direction is the easiest: the assumption that race is an observable physical fact, a thing, rather than a .... that is profoundly and in its very essence ideological.'
Barbara J. Fields, 'Ideology and Race in American History', 144.

'Ideas about color, like ideas about anything else, derive their importance, indeed their very definition, from their context. They can no more be the unmediated reflex of psychic impressions than can any other ideas. It is .... that tells people which details to notice, which to ignore, and which to take for granted in translating the world around them into ideas about the world.'
Barbara J. Fields, 'Ideology and Race in American History', 146.

notion

ideological context

The students' first task is to collect a certain number of cards in each category (say ten). The second task is to fill in the gaps in the text drawing on the word cards collected. This part of the game forces the students to engage closely with the text in order to supply the missing words. The groups score a point for each correctly matched pair. In the second round of the game, and using only the correctly matched cards, the groups formulate their own definitions of the concept and design a poster.

Outcomes and Reflections

Each group presents their poster and definition, describing the rationale behind its formulation. Others may ask questions, or challenge the presenters. The scoring is conducted anonymously whereby after each presentation, the teacher collects the scores from the observers and hands them to the presenting group. The presentation stage acts as feedback. The combined scores of the two rounds decide the winner.

iii. Who's the author?

Purpose and Aims

A variation on role-playing, the purpose of this game is to enable students to plan a brief seminar on a particular topic. Students can work in pairs or groups. The game gives them confidence in building arguments, engaging critically with a limited range of sources and consolidating knowledge of a set text.

Accessories

Thematic cards

Process

Present each pair or group with a set of thematic cards. The most important part is designing the cards in that they need to contain enough information to stimulate debate without being too revealing. There is a great scope for variety here and, depending on the context, cards could include theory, criticism, character traits, background information on authors, pictures and so on. There is no need to categorise the cards since each group will receive a complete set of ten cards. In the example given here, the students will grapple with the question of authorship. We would suggest playing the devil's advocate here and including a reference to a chosen author, possibly one that they are already familiar with, and his work. This should introduce an element of tangibility to an otherwise abstract exercise and invite the students to look at both sides of the argument and confront their assumptions about authorship.

Kazuo Ishiguro
- Born in Nagasaki, Japan on 8 November 1954
- In 1960 moved to Guildford, Surrey
- Attended Woking County Grammar School
- Travelled to America and Canada
- Graduated from University of Kent and gained Master of Arts Degree from University of East Anglia

A Pale View of the Hills
The Remains of the Day
The Unconsoled
Never Let Me Go
The Buried Giant
'A Family Supper'
'A Village after Dark'
Nocturnes: Five Stories of Music and Nightfall

'Literary texts do not exist on bookshelves: they are processes of signification materialized only in the practice of reading. For literature to happen, the reader is quite as vital as the author.'
Terry Eagelton, *Beginning Theory*, (1993),74.

'An author's intention is itself a complex text, which can be debated, translated and variously interpreted just like any other.
Meanings are not stable and determinate but are the products of language, which always has something slippery about it.'
Terry Eagleton, *Beginning Theory* (1993), 69.

'It is not the voice that commands the story; it is the ear.'
Italo Calvino, *Invisible Cities*, 106.

'We know that a text is not a line of words, releasing a single 'theological' meaning (the 'message' of the Author-God), but a multi-dimensional space in which a variety of writings, none of them original, blend and clash. The text is a tissue of quotations drawn from the innumerable centres of culture. '
Roland Barthes, 'The Death of the Author', *Image Music Text*, 146.

'So here you are now, ready to attack the first lines of the first page. You prepare to recognize the unmistakable tone of the author. No. You don't recognize it at all. But now that you think about it, who ever said this author had an unmistakable tone?'
Italo Calvino, *If on a winter's night a traveller*, 9.

'But then you go on and you realize that the book is readable nevertheless, independently of what you expected of the author, it's the book in itself that arouses your curiosity; in fact, on sober reflection, you prefer it this way, confronting something and not quite knowing yet what it is.'

Italo Calvino, *If on a winter's night a traveller*, 9.

The term intentional fallacy refers to 'the widespread assumption that an author's declared or supposed intention in writing a work is the proper basis for deciding on the meaning and the value of that work.'

Oxford Concise Dictionary of Literary Terms

'[A] text is made of multiple writings, drawn from many cultures and entering into mutual relations of dialogue, parody, contestation, but there is one place where this multiplicity is focused and that place is the reader, not as was hitherto said, the author.'

Roland Barthes, 'The Death of the Author', *Image Music Text*, 148.

Now, allow pairs or groups five minutes to familiarise themselves with the cards, look for connections and so on, after which they are given a question, for example: 'Is the author necessarily dead? Discuss in relation to Ishiguro's 'A Family Supper''. Of course, the students should already be familiar with the text under discussion. At the end of the activity, each group or pair prepares a quick presentation for the rest of the class. The presentation time can be divided between group members so that everyone gets a chance to speak.

Outcomes and Reflections

After the presentation, initiate discussion about what students found challenging in teaching the topic, what they had to overcome etc. To increase the level of difficulty, each group could be given specific instructions relating to the age, experience or knowledge base of their prospective students. Each group's presentation is scored anonymously by the other groups and winner selected at the end of all the presentations.

Variations

Try devising a different question for each group in order to vary the arguments presented.

iv. Building concepts

Purpose and Aims

To foster the ability to work with abstract concepts. The game encourages cooperation and independent thinking within a group environment. It aids in building confidence in formulating hypotheses while working with a defined pool of sources and helps to consolidate existing knowledge.

Accessories

Thematic cards, a board, dice, counters, a blank sheet of paper for designing a poster, marker pens, Blu-Tack etc.

Process

Students work in groups, and each group is handed a board, cards and the requisite number of counters. For the purposes of this game, a simple board with different colour squares will suffice. The colours of the squares correspond to the thematic categories of cards which demonstrate the evolution of the concept. Let us imagine a seminar introducing the concept of otherness as viewed through class stereotype. The game will need to demonstrate and teach the students how to view the idea of class discursively and critically. The more diverse the card categories the more challenging the task will be. In this scenario, the students will play with three categories: pictures, excerpts from critical sources, and quotations from literary texts. Here are some examples to give you an idea of the information contained in each category.

The 'underclass':
'Representations of this population as alternately real subjects and imagined grotesque terrors, rendered in depictions that purposefully resist making clear distinctions between one and the other, are fundamental to the popularity of inner-city scenes in newscasts, reality shows, and fictive media such as films and novels.'
John Hartigan Jr, *Odd Tribes*, 34.

'[S]tereotypes of 'hillbillies' are replete with references to dangerous and excessive sexuality; rape (both heterosexual and homosexual), incest, and sexual abuse are supposed to be common practices among poor rural whites.'
Annalee Newitz & Matthew Wray, 'What Is 'White Trash'?', 171.

Myrtle Wilson: 'I heard footsteps on a stairs and in a moment the thickish figure of a woman blocked out the light from the office door. She was in the middle thirties, and faintly stout, but she carried her surplus flesh sensuously as some women can. Her face, above a dark spotted dress of dark blue crepe-de-chine, contained no facet or gleam of beauty but there was an immediately perceptible vitality about her as if the nerves of her body were continually smouldering. [...] Then she wet her lips and without turning around spoke to her husband in a soft, coarse voice.'

F. Scott Fitzgerald,
The Great Gatsby, 28-29.

Daisy Buchanan: 'I looked back at my cousin who began to ask me questions in her low, thrilling voice. It was the kind of voice that the ear follows up and down as if each speech is an arrangement of notes that will never be played again. Her face was sad and lovely with bright things in it, bright eyes and a bright passionate mouth – but there was an excitement in her voice that men who had cared for her found difficult to forget: a singing compulsion, a whispered 'Listen,' a promise that she had done gay, exciting things just a while since and that there were gay, exciting things hovering in the next hour.'

F. Scott Fitzgerald,
The Great Gatsby, 12.

To begin the game, a player rolls a die and, depending on which square s/he lands, s/he picks up a corresponding card and reads it. The aim of this stage of the game is to collect a full set of cards, which comprises of two cards in each category. Once a group has collected a full set, they raise their hands and the game stops for everybody. The students then begin to examine the cards and formulate their own definitions of the concept, which they will later present as posters. This stage of the game will last approximately 20 minutes, after which the groups display their posters in the classroom to demonstrate their work.

Outcomes and Reflections

Since groups evaluate one another's posters, scoring serves as a reflective stage of the game. The card collecting stage of the game and poster stage are scored separately. For each card collected, the group is awarded a point. Posters are scored on their persuasiveness, on a scale from 1 to 5, 1 being the least persuasive (alternatively, this is a good opportunity to employ the actual marking criteria you use for formal assessments). When awarding a mark, each group will need to justify their judgement. The points are then added and the group with the highest overall score wins.

v. Racing

Purpose and Aims

The aim of the game is to help students understand ideologically charged concepts, for example the construct of race, and enable them to apply this understanding to literary interpretation. The game encourages critical engagement with texts, including the formulation and presentation of arguments, assists in building confidence and promotes cooperation.

Accessories

Cards, a board, counters, dice, a blank sheet of paper for designing a poster, markers, Blu-Tack etc.

Process

The game may be played in pairs or small groups and utilises a simple board. Each group is given a board, three sets of cards, counters, a die as well as paper and markers. The discrete card categories correspond to the colours of squares on the board and may include, for example, contemporary definitions of race, historical accounts of race, quotations from literary texts containing the word 'race' and pictures. Students are likely to have formed their own ideas of race. Now, they will learn to examine these ideas within a broader socio-cultural and literary context. Here are some examples of cards in each category:

'They are at least as brave, and more adventuresome [than whites]. But this may perhaps proceed from a want of fore-thought, which prevents their seeing a danger till it be present. When present, they do not go through it with more coolness or steadiness than the whites. They are more ardent after their female: but love seems to be with them more an eager desire, than a tender delicate mixture of sentiment and sensation.'
Thomas Jefferson *Notes on the State of Virginia* (1782), p. 142.

'[R]ace is given meaning through the agency of human beings in concrete historical and social contexts, and is not a biological or natural category'.
David Roediger, *Towards the Abolition of Whiteness*, 2.

'[W]hile race is ideologically constructed, it is constructed from real, predictable, repeated patterns of life'.
David Roediger, *Towards the Abolition of Whiteness*, 5.

'Those who live in a cold climate and in [northern] Europe are full of spirit, but wanting in intelligence and skill.'

Aristotle, *Politics*, 270.

'"Well, those books are all scientific", insisted Tom, glancing at her impatiently. "This fellow has worked out the whole thing. It's up to us who are the dominant race to watch out or these other races will have control of things".'

F. Scott Fitzgerald,
The Great Gatsby, 16.

'I stared at him and then at Tom, who had made a parallel discovery less than an hour before – and it occurred to me that there was no difference between men, in intelligence or race, so profound as the difference between the sick and the well.'

F. Scott Fitzgerald,
The Great Gatsby, 132.

In the centre of the board is placed a larger card, face down, which contains the question to be debated, for example: 'How does *The Great Gatsby* interrogate the concept of race?' It may also contain an extract from a given text or a short poem. The students are not allowed to look at this card until the first round of the game has been played. The students move around the board, collecting cards. The aim of this part of the game is to collect as many cards as possible as quickly as possible. Bearing this in mind, this round should either last a certain amount of time, or until a full set of cards has been collected, for example: three in each category. If a group collects a full set, they raise their hands and the game stops for everybody. The students look at the cards to see if they can discover connections between historical, literary and contemporary conceptions of race. Next, they turn to the card in the centre and, drawing on the information from the collected cards, they formulate a response and record their findings on the blank sheet of paper provided. This can be done in bullet points, diagrams etc. The posters are then displayed to the whole class.

Outcomes and Reflections

Each group presents their findings to the rest of the class. The presentation should include reflections on the process; what they found challenging about the question in relation to the studied text. Presentations are scored on their persuasiveness and, as in the previous game, the combined score for the card-collecting stage and presentation decides the winner.

Variations

To spice the game up, try introducing an additional set of cards. These could be multiple-choice cards which contain, for example, historical facts (note that the answer should not be read out immediately!):

Britain passed the Slavery Abolition Act in:

a) 1750

b) 1807

c) 1833

Answer: c

Columbus discovered America in:

a) 1507

b) 1492

c) 1825

Answer: b

A fellow group member collects a card and reads its contents to the student whose turn it is to roll the die. The student must answer the question correctly to execute her/his move. If an incorrect answer is given, s/he forfeits the move. This provides an interesting way of introducing historical context into the debate as well as injecting competition. It also transforms the simple task of collecting cards into a knowledge-broadening activity.

To set the debate within a broader theoretical and historical context, the card categories may include contemporary definitions of race and accounts contemporaneous with the text under discussion. Next, the students are asked to examine how, through character construction and character relations, the text intersects with or challenges the historical and contemporary conceptions of race. As before, they record their findings on the blank sheet of paper and present them to the whole class.

vi. Association/definition

Purpose and Aims

To facilitate the formation of ideas while cementing existing knowledge and promoting independent thought.

Accessories

A simple board, dice, multiple-choice cards, blank sheets of paper and writing implements.

Process

Working in groups, students take turns drawing cards. A player selects a card and reads it aloud. Aside from the question or statement, each card contains potential answers. The player next to him has to answer the question or complete the sentence. If he guesses correctly, he throws the die and moves on the board; if he guesses incorrectly, the game passes to the next player and so on, while the card is either returned to the bottom of the deck, or the question passes to the next player. Here are some examples of cards designed for a seminar introducing the students to the question of feminism and feminist criticism.

Feminism is:

a) a political stance

b) a form of literary criticism

c) both

Answer: both

Feminism is 'a political perception' which postulates 'that gender difference is the foundation of a structural inequality between women and men, by which women suffer systematic social injustice'.
Pam Morris, *Literature and Feminism*, 1.

True or False

Answer: True

Feminism argues that 'the inequality between the sexes is not the result of biological necessity but is produced by the cultural construction of gender differences'.
Pam Morris, *Literature and Feminism*, 1.

True or False

Answer: True

Biological essentialism assumes that physical differences between men and women determine their social roles and characteristics.

True or False

Answer: True

For each question answered correctly, the player keeps the card and the team is awarded a point. This is the first round of the game which is to be played dynamically. Only when everybody in a group reaches the finish line is the team given the next problem to solve. In this scenario, to stimulate conceptualisation, a general question will suffice, for example: 'Is feminism an anti-male movement? Discuss.' On the basis of the information gathered, the students prepare their response which they present to the class. The presentations are scored anonymously and the combined scores for the first and second round will decide the winner.

Outcomes and Reflections

The first stage of the game provides instant feedback to the students and an opportunity to correct their misconceptions or fill gaps in their knowledge; while the exposure to the other groups' presentations allows for reflection on each group's individual output.

Variations

To increase the spirit of competition, following the first round a winner could be selected from among the teammates in each group. To broaden the scope of the questions and increase the level of difficulty, a caveat may be added whereby more than one answer to each question may be possible. Effectively, this part is transformed into a trivial-pursuit/brainstorming hybrid.

You can make the game text-specific, in which case the information on cards, aside from theory, will include quotations from a particular text. It is therefore important that it is detailed and varied enough to test students' knowledge of the text and prepare them to compose an answer to the overarching question which will be revealed at the end, for example: 'Is Fitzgerald's Tom Buchanan an irremediably contemptible character?'

Yet another variation may dispense with the board and, instead, the students are presented with a quotation followed by a question, both cut up into words and placed on the table, face down. The game proceeds as before, with students taking turns to answer questions, as above. For each correctly answered question, they keep the card and uncover one word from the pile in the centre. This round stops when all the pieces of the quotation and question have been revealed. Then the students arrange them in order and, drawing upon the cards collected, they proceed to discuss it and present their findings to the group.

This scenario is adaptable to both debating general concepts and specific texts. It is necessary, however, that the information on the cards be thematically linked to the overarching question so that students are building up a context while playing.

vii. Mix & Match

Purpose and Aims

To facilitate understanding of socially and culturally constructed concepts such as femininity. The game encourages close engagement with literary texts and, through the reapplication of concepts, highlights their artifice.

Accessories

Excerpts from a text, blank sheets of paper, marker pens.

Process

This example is taken from *Pride and Prejudice*. The students work in groups and are presented with excerpts from the novel in which Mr Darcy muses on femininity. Looking at these, they produce a version of Mr Darcy's idea of the perfect woman (you could try some rogue cards and base a competition on which groups spot them). Next, they're presented with a question: 'What would Mr Darcy make of Bridget Jones as a woman?' Referring to Mr Darcy's ruminations, they produce his response and highlight which of Bridget's characteristics could awaken his pride or indeed prejudice. These are then presented to the class and scored on persuasiveness.

Outcomes and Reflections

In subjecting the construction of femininity to close scrutiny, the students explore the influence of societal expectations that lead to the emergence of gender roles. To reinforce the point, pose a simple question after the presentations: 'Is femininity a male invention?'

Variations

Try a flipped version of the game in which one of the female characters of *Pride and Prejudice* scrutinises the idea of a modern man. End by asking the question whether masculinity is a female invention.

viii. Polar opposites?

Purpose and Aims

To promote the application of critical theory and stimulate critical thinking. This is a game of comparisons, the aim of which is to put to the test the notion of binary oppositions. It helps to build the students' confidence in working with literary theory to facilitate a better understanding of literary texts.

Accessories

Cards with characteristics and characters, task cards, blank sheets of paper, marker pens.

Process

Working in groups, the students are given strips of paper with a single characteristic on them and their first task is to divide them into two categories: hero or villain. This accomplished, they are presented with a question – 'every hero needs a villain: true or false?' – and a set of cards containing a number of characters from a given text. Looking at the characteristics in each category, they begin to assign them to each character. The chances are that none of these will neatly fit one category and the students should find themselves questioning the notion of opposition in character formation. In their presentations, they'll have to adopt a position in relation to the question posed at the beginning: either true or false.

Outcomes and Reflections

After the presentations, ask the students to consider whether the notion of opposition alone is capable of producing a valid reading. Thus moving from empirical evidence to theory, the students acquire a working knowledge of Structuralism and its shortcomings.

ix. Pictionary

Purpose and Aims

To stimulate conceptualisation and discussion. This is a multi-modal game that explores and challenges the students' assumptions about abstract concepts.

Accessories

Concept cards, dice, blank sheets of paper, a dry wipe board or flip chart.

Process

First, ask for a volunteer. Once the volunteer comes forward, tell the class that this person will act as a judge who will time each group. The class is then divided into groups. It is important that the groups are not seated too close to one another. Each group is given a card containing an aspect of the concept under discussion, which they'll be asked to draw. The groups are then allowed some time to discuss the cards and select the drawer. Once this has been accomplished, the judge quickly asks each team to roll dice to decide the order of drawing. Then the first team takes the stand. For instance, in an introductory lesson to Gothic, the students may begin by grappling with its stock imagery – ruins, dungeons, pursuit, ghosts, suspense, terror and the requisite villain and maiden in distress. They have a minute or two to illustrate the card. The judge decides when the drawing begins and ends. The other teams begin guessing and a team is only awarded a point when somebody guesses correctly. The team who scores the most points wins.

Outcomes and Reflections

The teacher poses a question leading to the unveiling of the overarching concept. The groups are encouraged to look at the drawings which remain displayed in the classroom, focusing on similarities and differences between one another's pictures and, taking these into account, produce a more comprehensive definition of the concept.

Variations

The game can be tailored to teach abstract concepts such as ideology, otherness, race and so on. It can also be adapted to a discussion of specific texts. In terms of the latter, it may be used to discuss the difference between visual representation and text, interpretation and so on, or the way in which text affects visual representation and vice versa. Some of the cards could contain very brief but significant passages from a particular text, for example. Another variation is also possible here, whereby all groups are given the same clues.

The chances are that the drawings produced will be significantly different, thus supplying food for thought. The idea of having, say, four strikingly different drawings of the same concept would in and of itself demonstrate the complexity of the idea and suggest the influence of social context on its conceptions.

x. Class race

Purpose and Aims

To foster an understanding of the constructedness of ideologically slippery terms like race and class as well as the interconnectedness existing between them. The game encourages engagement with theoretical material through close textual analysis and interpretation.

Accessories

Cards, a simple board, counters, dice, blank sheets of paper for posters, markers, Blu-Tack etc.

Process

As usual, the students work in small groups, take turns rolling the dice and moving around the board collecting cards. The cards contain definitions of both concepts with the words class and race missing; they are colour-coded, corresponding to the colours of squares on the board, but the categories remain unnamed. In the centre of the board is placed a card, face down, with the following inscription: class or race. Once the card-collecting round stops, the students uncover the card in the centre and proceed to fill in the blanks in definitions, using either class or race. Here's an example:

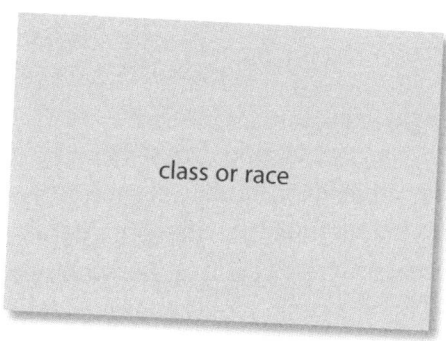

class or race

'[A]s a means of human classification, ... can ignore shared physical resemblance and categorise on the basis of assigned social legacy. Biological attributes – hair texture, eye color – gain significance from an intricate interweaving of history, ideology, and cultural practice.'
Valerie Babb,
Whiteness Visible, 10.

'At its core ... refers to a material circumstance: the inequality of human beings from the standpoint of social power.'
Barbara J. Fields, 'Ideology and Race in American History', 150.

Two ways of scoring are possible. Firstly, the answers to the matching round are revealed and students get a point for each correctly completed definition. Secondly, the presentations are scored on their persuasiveness. The combined scores decide the winner. It is worth noting, however, that placing emphasis on correct matching may be detrimental in this scenario as it may undermine the objective of the game, which is to demonstrate and understand the interchangeability of the two concepts. It may be more beneficial therefore to limit scoring to the poster round.

Outcomes and Reflections

Students look at the similarities and differences between class and race, and present their findings. The game demands a close engagement with text as its success is linked with noting the repetitious application of certain words (particularly adjectives) to perpetuate social and racial oppression through the construction of stereotypes.

Variations

This version of the race/class game revolves around a specific text. To facilitate this, another category of cards is introduced, bearing quotations from the text. Since the emphasis is on textual analysis, the definitions of the concepts are supplied. The card in the centre contains a specific question relating to a particular text, for example, *Great Expectations:* 'Pip – a social or racial inferior: discuss'. The students are implicitly given three options here which, to a degree, will depend on what quotations they draw: they can either discuss Pip in terms of class or race or, indeed, both.

To illustrate the correspondence between theory and social and cultural practices, not to mention the enhanced visual appeal of the game, why not add another category of cards depicting stereotypical representatives of class or race. For example:

The Irish declaration of independence that we are all familiar with

xi. People without shadows

Purpose and Aims

To foster critical engagement with literary theory through the application and questioning of its precepts – in this instance the notion of binary oppositions. This game allows the students to gain a practical knowledge of the theory and gives them an opportunity to test its limitations. It promotes close reading and argument building.

Accessories

Cards, excerpts from a text, blank sheets of paper.

Process

This game also revolves around a particular text and finding connections. Working in groups, the students are given a set of printed cards bearing the names of characters from a novel and a set of cards bearing their descriptions. There will be more characters than descriptions. First, they match characters to descriptions and then, from the remaining cards, choose their opposites. In the process, they will have to decide which character is the odd one out – the shadowless character without its opposite.

Outcomes and Reflections

They present their findings to the rest of the class, commenting on why the chosen character is shadowless. There is a relationship here to one of the precepts of Structuralism, namely the notion of oppositions as an organizing principle, and whether that defines or reduces the complexity of narrative.

5

Games about Developing Arguments

i. Challenge/solution

Purpose and Aims

To promote critical thinking, evaluation, discussion and building arguments. It enables students to develop lateral thinking and draw on existing knowledge. Group work stimulates confidence and naturally conditions the players to speak before an audience, progressing from the safety of the group to the class forum.

Accessories

Cards only.

Process

This game follows a challenge-solution pattern. It may be played in groups or pairs. Present the students with different categories of cards which, to make them more visually appealing, may be colour coded. The card categories may include, for example:

- Challenge cards – containing questions or contentious statements
- Suggestion cards – examples of texts for consideration. These will, of necessity, be limited to the curriculum material

- Miscellaneous cards – containing theoretical or historical information, depending on the theme of the lesson
- Idea cards – these will represent a hazard in that the information contained therein may be incorrect or misleading

Let's take as a seminar topic Jane Austen's *Pride and Prejudice* and its critique of society through the character of Mr Collins. In this scenario, the Challenge card will pose a specific question: 'Discuss the character and role of Mr Collins in *Pride and Prejudice*'. The Suggestion cards will contain quotations from the text pertaining to Mr Collins in an array of situations, for example:

'[Mr Bennet speaking of the letter he received] "It is from my cousin, Mr Collins, who, when I am dead, may turn you all out of this house as soon as he pleases".

"Oh, my dear" cried his wife, "I cannot bear to hear that mentioned. Pray do not talk of that odious man. I do think it is the hardest thing in the world, that your estate should be entailed away from your own children; and I am sure, if I had been you, I should have tried long ago to do something or other about it".'

Jane Austen,
Pride and Prejudice, 52.

'My mind however is now made up on the subject, for having received ordination at Easter, I have been so fortunate as to be distinguished by the patronage of the Right Honourable Lady Catherine de Burgh, widow of Sir Lewis de Burgh, whose bounty and beneficence has preferred me to the valuable rectory of this parish, where it shall be my earnest endeavour to demean myself with grateful respect towards her Ladyship, and be ever ready to perform those rites and ceremonies which are instituted by the Church of England.'

Jane Austen,
Pride and Prejudice, 53.

The scope of this question allows for the miscellaneous cards to include a mixture of theoretical and historical material, such as:

Entail: 'The settlement of the succession of a landed estate, so that it cannot be bequeathed at pleasure by any one possessor; the rule of descent settled for any estate; the fixed or prescribed line of devolution.'

OED

Gentleman: 'A man of superior position in society, or having the habits of life indicative of this; often, one whose means enable him to live in easy circumstances without engaging in trade, a man of money and leisure.'
Gentry: 'People of gentle birth and breeding; the class to which they belong; in modern English use *spec.* the class immediately below the nobility'

OED

The Idea cards in this instance may offer brief directions on how to approach the question, for example: 'Consider status and equality'; 'How does language reflect status?' and so on.

Before the game begins, divide the class into groups and ask each group to choose a representative. The representatives from each group approach a table and are instructed to select one card from the 'Challenge' pile, and a specific number of cards from the other stacks with the exception of Idea Cards. The representatives, without showing their Challenge cards to each other, return to their tables and present the cards to the rest of the group. The decision whether to request an Idea card is made at group level because all students are made aware of the dangers of Idea cards. Having all the accessories in place, the group then sets about answering the challenge question.

Since the representatives must not reveal the content of the challenge cards to each other, an element of secrecy is introduced into the game, which also means that the challenge cards may be identical. Once all groups have come up with their solutions, they are discussed at class level and the best option is selected. When presenting their solutions, groups are encouraged to describe the rationale behind them: the methodology of arriving at a particular solution. The presentations are scored anonymously and the highest score wins.

Outcomes and Reflections

The very exposure to others' interpretation of an identical question will raise students' awareness of the malleability and plurality of interpretation, challenging the notion of a correct interpretation.

Variations

To adapt the game to the discussion of a single text, the Challenge cards may contain different, though thematically related, problems. For example, a discussion of the constructions of manliness in *Pride and Prejudice* could involve each group discussing a different character. As a result, a more comprehensive picture of the overarching issue would emerge at the end of the session.

Another variation may involve all groups working with the same challenge question, but different tools. In this case, cards are arranged in sets and, perhaps, numbered. Each group rolls dice and selects the card set with the corresponding number. The remainder of the game proceeds as before.

This tiered approach lends itself easily to yet another variation. The representatives of each group collect challenge cards only, which they show to their group members. Working individually first, each student in a group drafts a plan of how the issue may be approached. Then, students within each group form pairs and then fours, all the while comparing their drafts until only one proposal remains. This centripetal movement promotes critical engagement with the question through the process of selection and fosters discussion. After choosing their final plan, each group receives the remaining source materials and, drawing on both, they develop a response to the set question and present it to their peers. To ensure the success of this scenario, all groups should contain an even number of players, ideally no more than four.

ii. Questions and answers

Purpose and Aims

To aid building arguments, stimulate conceptualisation and promote group discussion. Its gradual approach encourages confidence in presenting arguments.

Accessories

Simple board, theme cards, dice.

Process

Using a very simple board, students begin by rolling a die and, depending on which field they land, they either collect a bonus, move to another field, or incur penalty points, such as moving back to start, losing a turn or having to answer a question. Questions are provided on separate cards so as the board can be utilised in different scenarios. There is also a question placed face down in the centre of the board, and every time a student answers a question correctly, a piece of the overarching question is revealed. The questions should be designed in such a way as to introduce context for the overarching question. For example, to create context for the question whether *The Great Gatsby* is a tragedy, the supporting questions may concern character construction, motivation, and the conflict between ideality and reality:

Tragedy: 'a serious play (or, by extension, a novel) representing a disastrous downfall of a central character, the protagonist.'

Oxford Dictionary of
Literary Terms

Tragic flaw: 'the defect of character that brings about the protagonist's downfall in a 'tragedy': Othello's jealousy is a famous example. The idea of the tragic flaw involves a narrowing and personalising of the broader Greek concept of *hamartia* ('error' or 'failure').'

Oxford Dictionary of
Literary Terms

Ideality: 'Something which exists only as a mental conception; something ideal or imaginary; an idealized conception; The quality of being an ideal or idealization; ideal or imaginative character; *Philos.* The quality of being an abstract idea; imaginary or non-real nature; existence in idea only (opposed to *reality*).'

OED

'If personality is an unbroken series of successful gestures, then there was something gorgeous about him, some heightened sensitivity to the promises of life, as if he were related to one of those intricate machines that register earthquakes ten thousand miles away.'

F. Scott Fitzgerald,
The Great Gatsby, 4.

'No—Gatsby turned out all right at the end; it is what preyed on Gatsby, what foul dust floated in the wake of his dreams that temporarily closed out my interest in the abortive sorrows and short-winded elations of men.'

F. Scott Fitzgerald,
The Great Gatsby, 4.

As play unfolds, the students retain the card questions answered correctly so that there is a sense of winning and competition created. This round continues until all the pieces of the overarching question have been revealed. Now, the groups proceed to answer the question, drawing on the material collected during the first round.

Outcomes and Reflections

The discussion is then taken to the next level, the class forum, where the groups present their answers. The feedback generated thus allows for the broader understanding of a given text, reinforcing the idea of multiplicity of interpretation.

Variations

For an even more comprehensive engagement with a text, why not make the overarching questions different for each group while the background information remains the same.

iii. Adopting viewpoints

Purpose and Aims

To encourage debate and the formulation of hypotheses. The game allows the students to engage critically with a text, thus promoting interpretative skills.

Accessories

Cards, passages from a text, blank sheets of paper, marker pens.

Process

Although the students will eventually work as a group, initially this game begins at individual level. Each player is given a set of cards containing different viewpoints on a particular topic. It is important that the cards contain contentious information that will naturally stimulate discussion. One player, unbeknownst to her/him, will act as a mediator and route-setter for the debate. To this end, her/his cards will contain information relating to the direction the debate is to take. For example, if the objective of the lesson is to teach about polysemy, the cards could contain information on the nature of interpretation, language, character construction and so on. They begin by examining the cards and listing evidence to support their standpoint. After this stage is completed, the game moves on to the group level. The students read out their viewpoints and justify them. Their first task as a group is to see whether a consensus is possible, and if it is, what concessions and/or qualifications it may involve. This stage naturally promotes a deeper engagement with the issue at stake. Next, they are presented with a question and passage from a particular text and, bearing in mind how they've proceeded up to this point, are to present potential interpretations and justify them.

Outcomes and Reflections

By way of feedback, the students demonstrate their findings at a class forum and are scored on persuasiveness. Providing each group with score sheets containing marking criteria beforehand will naturally encourage reflection on each presentation.

Variations

Try the game with a simple board. This time, however, the students begin work as a group. Throwing dice and moving around the board, they collect seemingly contradictory statements on a particular topic or text. In the place of the route-setter, a set of red cards is introduced with suggestions how the statements may be approached. These are collected by landing on red marked squares on the board. Once all the red cards have been collected, this round stops and the conceptual part begins.

iv. Talking back

Purpose and Aims

To aid confidence in building and presenting arguments. The game fosters discussion and tests students' knowledge of both text and context.

Accessories

Text specific cards, thematic cards, blank sheets of paper, dice.

Process

Cards highlighting aspects of a text are dealt out to each student within a group. These cards constitute a mixture of text-specific extracts and thematic cards which may be reused in different scenarios. The latter could be topically general, something along the lines of dominant characters, political stance, physical setting, actions, lexis, idea vs. will (the general idea underpinning the text and its execution through characters' actions) and so on. Each student makes a note of their first response to the cards and proceeds to discuss them with the group, after which the whole group constructs their own counter-narrative. All groups work with the same sets of cards. Then dice are thrown to choose which group goes first to present their narrative.

Outcomes and Reflections

After each presentation, and before scoring, the students from the remaining groups are encouraged to pose questions. Each presentation is scored by the other groups (again, you could use standard assessment criteria) and the winner of the debate selected at the end. Scoring can be anonymous to encourage objectivity, whereby each group writes the score on a piece of paper and places it face down. The tutor collects the scores at the end of each presentation and announces the winner at the end.

v. Applying pressure

Purpose and Aims

To facilitate creation of arguments and counter-arguments. Adopting the notion of applying constant pressure such as the students would face if engaged in an actual debate, the activity naturally promotes discussion.

Accessories

Cards, blank sheets of paper.

Process

Students work in groups, subdivided into pairs. A group is divided into two pairs, and each pair is given a set of cards. These cards represent opposing points of view. It's good to choose contentious topics. One set of cards represents a positive standpoint, the other its opposite. Still working in pairs, they familiarise themselves with the cards and prepare an argument. The other pair does the same. The objective of the game is to keep up a constant exchange of information. The two pairs face each other and the exchange begins. The pair who runs out of things to say loses. Then the pairs switch cards and their task now is to put a negative spin on the positive cards and vice versa. Again, the pair who runs out of arguments loses.

Outcomes and Reflections

Following the exchanges, the members of each group reflect on which aspects of the process they found difficult and which easy. The experiences are discussed at the class level, with other groups invited to offer suggestions and solutions.

Variations

The game mechanics are easily adaptable to different thematic scenarios, including debates on specific literary texts. Again, deliberately provocative statements help (*Macbeth* is about the fear of terrorism' etc.).

vi. Snake/ladder

Purpose and Aims

To allow the students to practise argument-building while consolidating their knowledge of a given text or texts.

Accessories

A snakes and ladders board (a simplified version will suffice), dice and a set of quotation cards.

Process

The game may be played in pairs or in groups of four whereby two pairs play against each other. The scenario described here is based on a group of four. Depending on the topic, the cards can contain single words, statements and quotations. Pairs take turns rolling the dice and moving around the board collecting cards. The idea is to collect as many cards as possible; each card collected earns one point. There are two possibilities here: this part of the game may either continue for a fixed amount of time after which the points are added up, or until one pair reaches the finish line. The latter would be more gamely, of course, and if the board is a simplified version of snakes and ladders, reaching the finish line shouldn't take too long. Once one of the pairs has reached the finish line, this part of the game stops for the group. Then, the team is presented with a question or a statement, for example: 'Jane Austen satirizes all human society and all individuals'. The pair who gained the most points for the first round decides whether they want to endorse the statement or argue against it. If they decide to endorse it, the other pair is left with no option but to argue against it. Now, working in pairs they draft their responses and, after a set time, they begin to debate them with the other pair. Whoever devises the longest list of relevant arguments, either pro or against, wins.

Outcomes and Reflections

The winning pairs from each group compete against one another, while the spectators score them and a class winner is selected. Throughout the process, the students are able to observe the efficacy of their arguments, thus receiving instant feedback.

Variations

The game proceeds as above with the exception that the direction of the argument is predetermined. This will involve rephrasing the question, for example: 'Why isn't Jane Austen a satirist?' An alternative version is also possible without changing the rules much. Instead of one set of cards, there are two, each a different colour. One colour contains potentially contentious information in that it may be used in support of either argument. Depending on the topic, the information contained therein may relate to historical background, author, theory and so on; while the other could contain quotations only. In this scenario, the students end up with a variety of cards which they need to interpret to respond to the question.

vii. Building proofs

Purpose and Aims

To engage lateral thinking and cross-application of existing knowledge, as well as promote social interactions between players and discussion.

Accessories

A simple board, cards, dice and counters.

Process

Each group selects a representative who will compete against the other representatives. The representatives gather around a table with the board and begin by rolling a die to determine the order in which they will proceed to move. The board contains colour-coded squares that correspond to different categories of cards. Each representative rolls the die and, depending on which square s/he lands, s/he selects a card. The colour-coded cards represent different categories: theory, history, relevant contextual information, information about authors, and information related to relevant texts. This stage of the game should be played very quickly. Once a representative collects a requisite number of cards, for example two or three in each category, s/he draws or is given a question card and rejoins her/his group; the game continues for the other representatives. The groups evaluate the materials and have to produce a plan detailing how they would discuss their question, drawing upon the information they have gathered. They should include a rationale for their argument. At the end, they produce a poster to present their findings.

Outcomes and Reflections

The need to include a rationale behind their arguments in the presentation forces the students to engage critically not only with the material provided, but also with their response to it. It encourages an active evaluation throughout the process which culminates in the debriefing stage that is the poster presentation.

Variations

Getting the groups to work with the same problem question, unbeknown to one another, will demonstrate that there are no right or wrong answers; an empirical way of illustrating the idea of the multiplicity of interpretation. To spice up the game, and if you're technologically minded, you may try including a bonus square that would carry with it a card with a QR code. The information contained in it may be accessed when the representatives rejoin their groups.

This option, however, entails additional cost and labour outlay and relies on the students' possessing accessories capable of reading the codes. Perhaps a less exciting variation, because without the board, may involve the representatives' collecting pre-prepared sets of cards, i.e. yellow, red, green and purple. Unbeknown to the groups, despite the different colours, all sets contain the same information with the exception of the question they have to answer, or vice versa.